WRITING
the
MODERN
CONFESSION
STORY

by

DOROTHY COLLETT

Boston
THE WRITER, INC.
Publishers

Library of Congress Catalog Card Number: 73-142594
ISBN: 0-87116-010-2

PRINTED IN THE U.S.A.

CONTENTS

v

INTRODUCTION

The first magazine to feature the sin-suffer-repent story came into existence in 1919. By 1945, when I sold my first confession story, the big, wide-open confession market was flourishing. In the twenty years since I wrote the original *Writing the Confession Story*, in spite of drastic, world-wide changes that stagger the imagination, the confession magazines have continued to flourish, taking in an estimated $40 million in newsstand and subscription sales, according to a recent article in *The Wall Street Journal*.

There are several reasons for the solid, continuing popularity of the confession story, one of which is its successful fusion of fact and fiction. The "fact" story is found everywhere — in the true life experience, which can run the gamut from the "confession" of an individual who crossed the Pacific Ocean in a rowboat to the "confession" of a woman who, while lost in the woods during a blizzard, delivered her own baby. Fact stories are found in biographies, which can be written by professional biographers, the personal secretaries or the cooks of celebrities; and in autobiographies, which can be written by the famous personage himself or by a professional writer whose name is prefaced with: *as told to!* Then there's the straight article, which abounds in all magazines. This kind of essay states a premise that can deal with medicine, psychiatry, education, adolescence, poverty, prosperity, travel, or you-name-it, and then proceeds to illustrate its proposition with one or more *case histories.* These are examples of the popular "fact" piece.

As everyone knows, a piece of fiction is a neat contrivance that embodies certain interest-holding ingredients, such as an intriguing problem, conflict, suspense, likable characters, and so forth, all neatly and expertly culminating in a satisfying ending, with all the loose ends logically explained.

So isn't it obvious that the combined appeal of fact and fiction is unbeatable — with the reader getting his knowledge or his inspiration or help or encouragement while he is being entertained and satisfied?

Another big reason for the confession story's solid, continuing success is its high moral tone. True, the titles are often lurid, and the story content is frequently sensational, and even shocking. But the lesson is there. And the lesson is rigidly moral, with a wrong-doer being finally punished, with the right-doer being ultimately rewarded — and the basic tenets are a respect for God and Motherhood and Law and Country. The average, hard-working, decent men and women who read these stories are comforted and reassured by this uncompromisingly high moral tone, especially in these frightening, uncertain times.

Undoubtedly this continuing growth of the confession magazines is due in large part to the fact that they have

kept pace with the times. The quality of the writing in
them has steadily improved and is now comparable to the
writing in slick stories — often better, in my opinion. The
content is increasingly sophisticated, keeping pace with
changes in sex mores, education, controversy. Nowadays
the confession narrator may indulge in pre-marital sex without any punishment at all, let alone having this ruin her
whole life. The average narrator, male or female, more frequently than not goes to college as a matter of course. A
confession story today can deal with a controversial issue —
such as a racial problem or drug abuse or rioting or any
other form of violence that is part of our daily experience.
The confession magazines require their writers to keep up
with the times, whether we're at war or at peace, in depression or inflation. Now we have birth control pills and
vital organ transplants and a whole generation of children
who are strangers to their parents. Who knows what we'll
have tomorrow? Because of the tremendous progress in
communications, the awareness of the average Mrs. Every-
woman who reads the confession stories has expanded
enormously in every direction. We have a whole new vo-
cabulary since a decade ago. And all these current *happen-
ings* are faithfully reflected in the mature confession story
of today.

Who are these readers? *The Wall Street Journal* says that
confession magazines sell ten million copies a month
to salesgirls, typists, dressmakers, and other working class
women; middle-class housewives like to read them, and
their husbands often browse through their wives' copies. In
analyzing the readership of confessions, they conclude: Men

comprise 17% of the 18-years-and-over group; 56% of the women readers are 18 to 34; 23% are 35 to 49; 21% are 50 and over. The substantial under-18 group is uncounted.

Who are the writers? *The Wall Street Journal* further divulges the fact that one consistently selling confession writer is a male inmate of the Ohio Penitentiary, serving a 10-to-25 year sentence for armed robbery. It cites the case of a former high school English teacher who, with his wife, sold 88 confession stories in one year, and they consistently make enough money to support themselves and their four children.

Among the many confession writers I know personally there is a widow who was left financially well off, but who writes confession stories to finance her trips around the world. Another woman, who has been writing them for twenty-five years, has earned enough to support an ailing husband and two children. I know elderly and young people who write confessions, some with impressive academic degrees, some with very little formal education. I know men who write them — and young girls. And great-grandmothers! The variety of people who write confession stories is tremendous.

What does all this mean? It means that the confession field is a wonderful way to make a living for anyone who has the ability to write an interesting letter — and who is willing to learn the rules.

And that's what this book is all about — those rules!

WRITING THE MODERN
CONFESSION STORY

CHAPTER I

THE CONFESSION MARKET

I want to start out with an earnest warning for all those who sincerely intend to write a confession story: Disregard everything in the way of advice and comment on confession stories from anyone who does not write confessions, or who does not regularly read these stories because she enjoys them, or who does not work in the editorial office of a confession magazine. Not only do such people know nothing about confessions, but — and this is what is so damaging to the sensitive, vulnerable, new confessions writer — they are invariably, *vocally* and condescendingly positive they know all about the confession field.

There is a tremendous number of such people, spieling off a frightening amount of misinformation. We've all met the man — over and over — who leers suggestively at you when you admit to being a confession story writer; who cracks the tired old joke, "And have you lived all these experiences you write about?" All you can do is yawn out the stock answer, "If I had, I wouldn't have had time to write about them." He will let out an appreciative guffaw, and you will silently resolve never to admit again what your lucrative, enjoyable vocation is! We've all met the young woman — or the older woman or the man of any age — who says, with a patronizing smile, "If I could ever find the time, I'd write a confession story — just to pick up some extra money, of course." You squirm, but all you can do is grit your teeth and try to find a grain of comfort in your secret knowledge that this person could never write one in a hundred years. We all know the ones who gasp in shocked horror, "You write those dirty things? How can you?" Or, with a fastidious shudder, "How can you read them? I'd be embarrassed to buy one." And so on, ad nauseum. We all know them. And you'll meet them! All I can do is prepare you for them and suggest that you remember Liberace's famous words — "I cry all the way to the bank."

This is not to say that the stories don't often promise sensational thrills, with their lurid titles and sexy blurbs plastered all over their covers. But look around at the covers on other kinds of magazines on your newsstand, and you'll realize this is par for the course these days. But the story title is only the bait. The most sensational bit in the story was probably selected for the tantalizing title. When you read the story, no matter how sensational the title or illustration or blurb, you will find that the narrator is basically decent and well-meaning, with emotions like yours. If she has "sinned" — and, since this is a confession story, she had better — she is surely going to be punished for it. And she is going to have to find some way to atone for it. And the reader can be sure that by the time she finishes the story, this "sinning" narrator has "reformed" for the rest of her life.

So, except for brighter, more garishly colored and wilder

"trimmings" to keep it up to date with the current "styles," the confession story is still, basically, the same solid, helpful, morally sound story it always was, with the same plot elements and the same writing "do's" and "don'ts." And with the same advantages for the writer!

Let's take a look at some of these advantages. First, there's an enormous need for the same type of confession story. One editor I know buys fifty stories a month. With approximately thirty confession magazines — the exact figure varies, but on a reliable in-and-out basis — each using from eight to twelve stories a month, this would indicate a buying market of approximately 300 stories a month. This means two things, both of which favor the writer. One, it means that his properly structured, typical confession story — as opposed to the occasional off-beat exception — can logically be marketed everywhere and conceivably bought by any one of these magazines. Two, it means that the editorial need for a good confession story is constant.

Another special advantage of the confession market to the beginner is the lack of a by-line. The main reason for this is the fact that so many of the readers like to believe that the story was actually written by the narrator of that story. And for those who don't believe this, the illusion must be kept intact for the all-important tone of reality. This means that an established name isn't important to the confession editor because she can't use it. She buys a story because she likes it and because she thinks her readers will like it. For the same reason, the beginner doesn't have the competition from the more experienced writer who wants to see his name in print.

The Story

Now that we've taken a close-up look at the confession *market*, let's take a closer look at the confession *story*. The dictionary defines the word confession as "a voluntary admission by a person who committed a crime." That's all right if we understand the elasticity of the word *crime* as applied to the confession story and range its meaning all the way from a not-quite-ideal-attitude to murder. So a more accurate definition for our purpose would be "a voluntary admission by an individual who has learned a lesson the hard way."

The first-person presentation is a rule without exception since, you will remember, it is the nature of the confession story to present itself as the narrator's own true experience. Although this can't be accepted in its most literal implication, the stories are true in the wider sense that the problems and situations and climaxes are real, because the author has — either consciously or subconsciously — drawn them from experiences of his own and of those he knows.

Men, women, boys, and girls "tell" these stories, though the proportion varies with the times. For instance, while it is possible today to write *and sell* a confession story that is narrated by anybody who is old enough to have lived and felt and written an interesting experience, *currently* there is a greater-than-ever demand for the man-woman story, with the emphasis on youth, with an element of violence more desirable than the story where nothing actually happens beyond a subtle change of heart on the part of the narrator.

Any properly executed confession story that deals with any problem that is at the present time relevant to the majority of the people who read these stories can be sold. But, again, the wise writer makes it his business to be sharply aware of the current trends and to slant his stories accordingly. He knows that sex, youth, and violence are "in" right now, and that means the editors are primarily interested in publishing stories that deal with sex, youth, and violence. Because the inclusion of one or more of these three ingredients in a confession story is so important *now*, and because it is *always*, at any time, an advantage to use them, a brief explanation of each, as applicable to the confession story, is in order here.

Sex. A sex story is not a story in which the author has deliberately injected sexy scenes to give it some zing; it is a story that is complete without the sex. The editors do not want stories with such overlaid, superficial, unnecessary sex scenes. A sex story is a story in which some aspect of sex is an *integral* part of the story, i.e., a sex *problem*. And the possibilities are endless. There's the frigid wife, for instance. Or the partner who suspects the other of homosexual or lesbian tendencies. Then, there's the Narcissus tendency, the sadistic, the masochistic, and the nymphomaniac — though I want to rush in with a word of warning here. *Abnormal* sex is not in as much demand among the buying confessions editors as is a fresh aspect of *normal* sex. And there's certainly an endless stream of possibilities here that you can keep using in new combinations. There's the wife with the straying husband and the husband with the wife who's had an affair with another man. There's the partner who's had surgery and feels sexless — and the mate who can't accept this in his partner. There's the partner with the insatiable sex needs, causing a problem for the mate, and there are all the unmarried variations. And this barely skirts the surface of all the available angles. Once the writer's attention is alerted in this direction, he'll keep reading and hearing and seeing things that will spark his imagination, and he'll be off with another plot idea to develop. One important caution about sex in confession stories — it must be done in good taste. This generally means handling it indirectly, implying rather than stating in so many blunt words, letting the reader's imagination fill in the words and pictures you have suggested but have *not* put into print.

Youth. A few years ago we read a lot of stories written by older narrators — elderly men and women with their problems of being unneeded, unwanted, shunted into retirement homes, grandmothers, mothers of teen-agers, older spinsters or widows looking for husbands, older wives worrying about unfaithful husbands, and so on. And quite possibly we will be reading great quantities of them again in a few years. But right now, even though we can still sell and read an occasional older-narrator story, the *now* emphasis is on youth — and this current trend is reflected in the confession story, with most stories nowadays narrated by *young* people — teens, young unmarrieds, young marrieds . . .

Violence. Again, the violence in the world is reflected in our stories, and the violent happening — the murder, beating, shooting, accident, rape, danger, threats, blackmail, hate, and so on — adds to the reality and the importance of your story. But, apart from the consideration of the timeliness, it is *always* better to have something big and bad *actually happen* as opposed to the *close-shave climax* that sold more readily a few years ago.

The main thing to remember is to keep reading the currently published confession stories. This is the most reliable way to get the feel of what's wanted *now,* whenever that *now* is!

Even though I've already touched on the purpose of the confession story, I want to elaborate a bit here. It must *entertain* — yes! The reader's interest must be aroused and sustained. But, while this is the whole goal of some stories, it is only a part of the purpose of the confession story. The confession story must also *inspire* the reader. This can mean a concrete solution to his or her problem or to the problem of someone close to him; or it might merely throw a new, encouraging light on it; or it can show those who are weighted down with burdens or drabness or despair that other people just like themselves have faced such hopelessness and have succeeded in overcoming it; or it might serve to prevent some from making serious mistakes by showing them in advance, through the experience your narrator is confessing, that the pitfalls are tragic and cannot be avoided; or it could demonstrate to others who have already made serious mistakes and paid for them that there is always another chance.

And for this very reason that all confession stories — despite their wide range of subject matter and the need to trim them with whatever type of embellishment is currently in fashion — do share the same ultimate purpose, it is possible to fit practically all of them into one basic pattern.

CHAPTER II

THE TEN ELEMENTS

The foundation for every typical confession story consists of the following ten elements:

I.   NARRATOR'S CHARACTER FLAW.

II.   MOTIVATION FOR NARRATOR'S CHARACTER FLAW.

III. DEVICE THAT CREATES NARRATOR'S IMMEDIATE PROBLEM AND NECESSITATES A DECISION OR PLAN.

IV.   NARRATOR'S WRONG DECISION OR PLAN.

V.   RESULT NARRATOR EXPECTS OR HOPES FOR.

VI.   ACTION RESULTING FROM NARRATOR'S DECISION OR PLAN.

VII. UNEXPECTED AND UNFORTUNATE RESULT OF THE ABOVE ACTION.

VIII. HOW THIS UNANTICIPATED RESULT CAUSES NARRATOR TO SEE WHERE AND WHY SHE WAS WRONG.

IX.   NARRATOR'S REMORSE AND HER ATTEMPT TO MAKE RESTITUTION.

X.   HOW NARRATOR'S REMORSE AND ATTEMPT TO MAKE RESTITUTION UNEXPECTEDLY BRING HER HAPPINESS, AFTER ALL.

Now let's consider these elements separately and in detail:

I. NARRATOR'S CHARACTER FLAW

"Flaw" covers that *fault* or *attitude* on the part of the narrator that is going to be overcome by the end of the story. The type of "flaw" varies in degree with the individual story.

A. The most common or typical *faults* include jealousy, envy, conceit, selfishness, fearfulness, wilfulness, stubbornness, greed, vanity, carelessness, irresponsibility, self-pity, snobbishness, and dozens more. Everyday faults that you find in everyday people in varying degrees.

B. A mistaken *attitude* usually applies to a specific issue, which would be the case with the narrator who was obsessed by a vicious hatred for an individual or a particular group — an ethnic group, for instance. Or with one who didn't want to get involved — or who couldn't mind her own business. Either way she can be wrong, depending on the plot development. Or at the other extreme, it would apply equally to the narrator who wasn't quite "big" enough to forgive wholeheartedly someone who had greatly wronged her; or to a narrator who felt that a great deal of money was essential to happiness.

If the narrator is unaware of the "flaw" all through the story, then you have the come-to-realize type of story: for example, your narrator thinks that keeping her husband satisfied in bed is all that is necessary to keeping him happy. So she, as narrator of your story, can't tell the reader that this is her "flaw." You, as creator of this story, have to give the reader evidences that show how this wife's *mistaken attitude* is wrong. Then, in the course of this story, your narrator continues to do her best in this direction and is completely baffled when her marriage begins to topple. She doesn't understand until the story climax, which forces her to see that sex is only *one* of a husband's needs — that a clean house and good meals, etc. also have their important place in a successful marriage.

On the other hand, if your narrator is perfectly aware of her "flaw" all along, then you have a story wherein the narrator reforms. Your narrator in this type of story might be a high school girl who is insanely jealous of her older, prettier, more popular sister. She knows she's jealous, and she admits it frankly to the reader, as she confesses her story. But, her point is, how can she help it when there is so much reason for it, etc. . . But, of course, you and the reader know that something (story climax) is going to cure her before the story is over.

II. MOTIVATION FOR NARRATOR'S CHARACTER FLAW

This is your narrator's past experience that has made her the way she is when your story opens and is almost always best given in *flashback* after your story is underway and your reader's interest is captured.

Now, keeping in mind the importance of reader-identification (making it possible for the reader to identify herself with the narrator), the narrator must be at all times sympathetic to the reader. Otherwise the reader won't particularly care what happens to the narrator; her fate and your story won't be important to the reader.

Therefore, you must show the reader how your narrator got this "flaw." Your motivation must justify this "flaw" so that the reader will think: "She's all wrong, but I'd probably be that way myself if I'd had that kind of life . . . " Or ". . . if I'd had an experience like that . . ." And when your reader reacts this way she's going to be very anxious to read on to see if everything is going to work out all right for this misguided narrator. The narrator has become real to the reader because you have established your conflict by giving your narrator a character flaw, which is obviously going to lead to trouble, and by justifying it so that your narrator is sympathetic and plausible and — in the heart of your reader — true to life.

Sometimes this element is very slight, and sometimes it is necessarily long and detailed with dramatic highlights, depending upon how much is necessary to make your particular narrator sufficiently sympathetic and real.

For instance, if your narrator is merely feeling a little rebellious because her husband's ex-wife is making unreasonable and unfair demands on his time and bank account, it obviously isn't going to take much motivation (or past experience explanation) to cause the reader to sympathize with her.

On the other hand, if your narrator is planning to murder someone who appears to be all right, then the reason behind this desire would have to be strong enough to make such a desire understandable. And generally this type of motivation requires a more dramatic flashback, so that the reader can live through it, too, and feel as strongly about it as the narrator does.

III. DEVICE THAT CREATES NARRATOR'S IMMEDIATE PROBLEM AND NECESSITATES A DECISION OR PLAN

This is usually the best place to open your story for reasons which will be discussed in a later chapter. The device is the incident you invent or the situation you create that results in an immediate problem.

This is the place where your narrator receives the news that the man who jilted her is coming back to town with his new wife. She is still in love with him, and now her own husband, whom she married as a better-than-nothing compromise, is unbearable to her. What is she going to do about it?

Or your device is an automobile accident, in which your beautiful, *engaged* narrator is injured in such a way that she will be unable to have children. This device has to pose an *immediate* problem, so perhaps she is engaged to a man who is *particularly* anxious to have many children of his own. Perhaps you can contrive the whole problem in such a way that he doesn't have to know the extent of her injury. What is *she* going to do?

Or maybe your narrator is a woman whose husband asks for a divorce (device). This narrator has known her husband was carrying on with his secretary, but she hasn't known what to do about it. There is their child to consider, but on the other hand there is her pride, too. (Your device has necessitated a decision or plan.) So now she *has* to do something. What is she going to do?

IV. NARRATOR'S WRONG DECISION OR PLAN

Is the jilted girl going to try to win him back? In spite of the fact that they are both married now? Does she justify her plan on the grounds that there are no children involved? Or is she just going to contrive to have an affair with him? Or does she plan a way to punish his wife?

And is the girl who can't have children now going to run away from her fiancé? Or is she going ahead with the marriage without telling him she can no longer bear children? Or do you want to complicate this story further by having her doctor fall in love with her? Or how about the man in the other car who caused the accident? Maybe he'll do anything she wants him to in order to make up for his guilt.

In the case of the woman whose husband wants a divorce — is she going to give it to him? Or is she going to refuse and hope for the best? Or is she going to get even with the secretary by publicly divulging the scandalous secret in the secretary's past that she has unearthed?

Before we can know what her decision is going to be, we have to know what her CHARACTER FLAW (*Element I*) is, because there must be a direct relationship between these two elements.

For instance, in the case of the jilted girl it was probably her CHARACTER FLAW (*Element I*) that caused the man to jilt her in the first place. And this same flaw (which she still has, because she hasn't learned her lesson yet) is going to influence her decision: i.e., if her flaw is wilfulness, then that is why he left her, and that would be why she would decide now to try to win him back. And it would be the reason for her present marriage going bad.

The same applies to the narrator who was injured. If her flaw is self-pity, then she would probably run away, feeling sure he couldn't want her now. If her flaw is a tendency toward trickery or deceitfulness, then she would decide not to tell him — with the idea of pretending ignorance when the time comes that he will have to know, or with the hope that once she is safely married he won't want to leave her.

And again with the narrator whose husband wants a divorce. Her CHARACTER FLAW (*Element I*) is probably the cause of this situation. Perhaps it is because she is so unreasonably jealous. If this is so, then she, suspecting the secretary, would probably take advantage of her chance to ruin the secretary's reputation. But maybe her flaw is a *mistaken attitude* toward their child. Maybe she feels that her first duty is to her child, regardless of her husband's need. Then, in view of her attitude of devoting herself so exclusively to her child, she would probably refuse, with the idea of keeping up a phony married "front" for the sake of the child.

But, whatever your narrator's decision is, you can see now that she isn't going to make the *right* decision or the *right* plan toward solving her problem *because* of her character flaw.

Since it would be too confusing for my purpose here to go on with the development of three stories at the same time, I'll proceed from here with just one of them. In this way I can show you how each element must necessarily influence the next element (so that your story will have unity, direction, and conviction), in addition to illustrating each of the remaining elements.

So let's settle on the narrator whose husband asks for a divorce. And let's say that her CHARACTER FLAW (Element I) is a *mistaken attitude* toward her baby, i.e., she puts the baby ahead of her husband, practically abandoning him in her possessive involvement with her baby. We know what her PROBLEM (Element III) is, but before we can be sure what her decision is going to be, we'll have to take time off to figure out how she acquired this flaw — or what it was in her past experience that led her into this present problem. So back to Element II. . . .

II. MOTIVATION FOR NARRATOR'S CHARACTER FLAW

Probably this narrator, as a girl, plans to have lots of children when she marries. And after she does marry, she feels even more sure that children are essential to a happy life. She and her husband are very much in love with each other though, and they are happy in spite of the fact that there aren't any children right away. However, she begins to get worried after the first year and consults her doctor. When he tells her she isn't likely ever to have any, she is heartbroken.

Her husband isn't so crushed by this news. Babies aren't such a major issue with him. His main concern is his wife's happiness.

Now he tries to comfort her. He tells her they can have lots of other things — a closer companionship than most couples, more shared experiences than couples with children, more fun together and more freedom.

She never gets over her disappointment, but she does see her husband's point. Since it can't be, she can at least have these other things. So for years and years she devotes herself — her time and thoughts and efforts and love — exclusively to her husband. He becomes the recipient of her frustrated mother instincts. And he loves it. And the fact that neither of them has any close relatives makes them even more dependent on each other.

Then after all these years of this close relationship, the unexpected happens. She is going to have a baby.

But it isn't smooth sailing, because of this difficulty — whatever it is — that has so long prevented her from having children.

And right here I want to digress for a minute to say that a story such as this will be immensely improved if you give the reader a medical explanation for this narrator's inability to conceive before, for finally conceiving now, and for the doctor's statement that she will not be able to have another. You occasionally read stories like this without the scientific fact to give it authority, but I personally wouldn't risk it. I would go to one of my "sources" for the medical condition that would serve this purpose. And all writers either have to do a certain amount of research or have a list of contacts for those occasional odd bits of legal or medical or geographical knowledge or whatever the specific story needs to give it authoritative credibility.

Going back to our story now, we'll say that all through the waiting period, she thinks of nothing else. Naturally this means a big readjustment in her marriage. This isn't so easy for her husband, under these circumstances, but he tries to be patient. After all, this unsatisfactory situation is bound to end — when the baby arrives. Then the baby is born. Delicate, premature! For a while it is touch and go. And this baby's life is even more important than ever, because it is the only baby she can ever have. (Remember — this was part of the doctor's explanation!)

All during the baby's first year, while she is completely wrapped up in him, her husband's bewilderment and resentment are increasing. The baby's needs and the baby's demands are constantly depriving him of all the happiness he has had before. His whole life is changed, and he is out in the cold.

(Don't forget that you, as author, must know *all* your characters. You must know at all times how their minds are working and why they are working that way — even though your narrator may not know. If you want your *reader* to understand a certain quality or reaction of one of the characters that your *narrator* does not understand, then you must see to it that your reader can *surmise* this quality or reaction through his actions, as the narrator reports them.)

And by the end of the baby's first year, the husband expresses his resentment in irritability, impatience with the baby, and frequent, unpleasant outbursts.

The narrator is equally bewildered — and equally resentful. She is beginning to realize that in the beginning when they thought they weren't ever going to have a baby it was only she who was so disappointed. He hadn't been! And now she concludes that he really didn't *want* a baby. He isn't happy, as she is, to make the endless sacrifices a baby requires. All he wants apparently is a combination of a gay, fun, sexy companion and an adoring woman to mother him. So, not understanding, she turns all the more toward the child and away from him.

And while things are gradually getting worse during the second year of the baby's life, her suspicions of his interest in his pretty, young secretary are growing. Let's say that our narrator has known for a long time that the secretary is in love with her husband. But it never bothered her before, because she was so sure of him. Now, however, she isn't sure, and things are all pointing in that direction. Perhaps she hears that they lunch together often. Then one night when she decides to meet him at his office, she sees them together in the parking lot. They are walking, arm in arm, whispering and laughing in an intimate, excited way. The narrator is glad they didn't see her. She's struck by the old, happy, boyish expression on his face which *she* hasn't seen for a long time. And perhaps the secretary herself is changed and now has that blooming look of one who is loved — or at least has hopes of it.

It is obvious that things can't go on like this indefinitely. And they don't! Finally there is the quarrel that ends all quarrels. Perhaps there is a company banquet where her husband is to receive some recognition. So they are planning to go in style. But at the last minute, the baby develops a sniffle. And the narrator won't leave him. Her husband is furious because the baby is interfering again, and the wife is putting the baby first. The narrator is angry and hurt because her husband is so lacking in affection for their child. It's the last straw!

Do you see that this MOTIVATION (Element II) has *explained* her CHARACTER FLAW (Element I) and brought it right up to date (and in *direct relationship*) with her PROBLEM (Element III)?

And do you see how this motivation for her flaw would be bound to influence directly her DECISION (Element IV) and the RESULT SHE EXPECTS (Element V) from this decision?

III. DEVICE THAT CREATES NARRATOR'S IMMEDIATE PROBLEM AND NECESSITATES A DECISION OR PLAN

Our device — the incident we have created to pose an immediate problem — is having the husband, who is completely fed up now, ask for a divorce.

Now she has to do something. Perhaps when he asks for his freedom, he assures her that he will gladly continue to support them in the style to which they have become accustomed. So, he goes on insultingly, unless they need him for something other than financial support, he would like to be free for a happier life elsewhere. Maybe she asks him if he's planning to marry his secretary. And maybe he coldly replies that he might!

If this is where you open this story — and this is where I advise you to open it — then this situation must be securely and dramatically established. When this is accomplished, we would swing back to Element II in its entirety but in a more brief and less dramatic style than we would use for the *present* part of the story. When this is done, we're ready to move forward into Element IV.

IV. NARRATOR'S WRONG DECISION OR PLAN

Our narrator in this story we're developing is angry and hurt and bitter, too. And she doesn't blame herself. She blames her husband. But, since the baby is her foremost consideration these days, she pauses to examine this angle. But he won't be losing much of a father, she reasons, in losing this one who seems to feel nothing but resentment toward his own child and who creates a constant atmosphere of friction — and who obviously wants someone else. Nor will the baby suffer any insecurity, since their financial support will continue. So it seems that in giving up the husband, she isn't really losing anything — except this atmosphere of friction. *So she decides to let him go!* (Of course pride enters into her decision, too, pride for herself and her child, but pride is only an outgrowth of her basic CHARACTER FLAW.)

V. RESULT NARRATOR EXPECTS OR HOPES FOR

Your narrator has made her decision or her plan, and now you must be very sure that you know exactly what she hopes will come of her plan — and very sure that you make it perfectly clear to the reader just exactly what she is hoping to gain.

Depending upon your individual story, this hoped for result can range from a negative to a positive form of reasoning; i.e., in one story the narrator merely chooses the lesser of two evils; in another story she has visions of her heart's desire when she makes her decision.

I'll illustrate this point with the case of a girl who loves a man who doesn't love her. He loves another girl, but he is unaware of her sordid secret. Narrator, however, had discovered this rival's shameful secret. This could be a prison record, for instance. Or an illegitimate baby whom she gave away or who died! (Narrator's discovery, incidentally, would be the device in this story; her problem is whether to keep the secret, as she had promised, or whether to expose it.) So this narrator decides to expose the secret.

Now if she knows that she herself can't have him whether he leaves this girl or not, then she is expecting only the satisfaction of revenge. But if she thinks he would turn to her if only he weren't so dazzled by this other girl, then she expects to achieve her complete happiness.

The important point here is that *you* know exactly what your narrator expects when she makes her decision and that you make sure your narrator expresses this expectation, so that the reader will know, too, however negative or positive the expectation might be. Your reader must have a clear-cut picture of the way your narrator's mind is working, so that she can follow along with her in perfect understanding. *This is how you achieve reader-identification.*

In our plot, then, our narrator expects to terminate an inharmonious environment for her child and herself, doesn't she?

VI. ACTION RESULTING FROM NARRATOR'S DECISION OR PLAN

This (Element VI) is usually the body of the story. Everything that happens as a result of the course your narrator has chosen belongs in this part of the story and leads directly up to the climax — or the UNEXPECTED AND UNFORTUNATE RESULT (Element VII) of this action. There are plots, however, to which this does not apply and which will be discussed in a later chapter. In *this* plot, as in most, this *is* the body of the story.

This is the part of the story where we would show the separation of the narrator and her husband, his moving out, then the waiting period before the court hearing. We would show how lots of ordinary, everyday little things are going wrong — the things which her husband had automatically taken care of before that she now has to attend to herself.

As time moves on, incident after incidents show that her chosen life of tranquility is not as tranquil as she had expected even though he is out of it. And of course she finds herself missing the sex, even though it was such a bore lately when he was around. Here, as she lies alone in bed, show her loneliness and the bewildering hunger, etc.

Then we would have one final incident that tops them all. Let's say she is taking down the screens — or putting them up, depending upon the season — when she falls from the ladder and hurts her back. Not seriously, because all we want to do is get her away from the baby for a while, but seriously enough so that the doctor orders her to the hospital for a couple of weeks.

The narrator calls on her friend (and remember this friend would have to be planted — woven into the story — earlier) to help her out in this emergency. The friend comes over to the narrator's house and agrees to take charge of the baby until she (friend) can locate a dependable, efficient woman for the job.

It doesn't occur to the narrator that her friend might call on the husband to help in this crisis, because the friend knows they're separated. But *you*, as the creator of all this, know — although the *reader* doesn't know yet, because the narrator can't tell the reader — that the friend isn't able to locate a nursemaid and something has to be done because the friend's own affairs are pressing. So you, the writer, know that the friend calls upon the estranged husband to get someone in this emergency. The friend probably personally feels that it is more his responsibility than hers, regardless of the narrator's feeling toward him. But the friend doesn't want to upset the narrator when rest and relaxation are so important to her recovery, so she calls the narrator at the hospital a couple of days later to report that everything is fine and that a very efficient and reliable person is now established in her home with her baby and there is nothing to worry about.

VII. UNEXPECTED AND UNFORTUNATE RESULT OF THE ABOVE
      ACTION

This is the climax of your story. This is the unfortunate result that your narrator didn't anticipate. This is what will keep the editor from rejecting your story as "too predictable." But remember — no matter how exciting or dramatic or surprising your climax is, it's no good if it doesn't *evolve logically* from all that has gone before — and if it doesn't serve to show the narrator where she has been wrong.

In this particular plot, the climax comes when the narrator gets home from the hospital and finds her baby in the care of her husband's secretary. While the secretary is explaining how it all came about (friend calling husband; husband unable to get nursemaid; finally asking her to pinch-hit), the narrator is getting angrier and angrier. It seems that the husband and the secretary have been taking turns at the office and taking care of the baby.

Narrator hurls an accusation at the secretary. She probably accuses her of not being satisfied with taking her husband — now she wants her baby, too!

Whereupon secretary lets narrator have it, too! She says maybe he won't love her as much as he once loved narrator, but at least she'll make him happier than narrator made him. And furthermore, secretary points out, now that the husband has had a chance to get acquainted with his baby (through no fault of narrator's) and now that he's had a chance to get used to the fact that narrator no longer loves him, he's begun to feel differently about his child. He's going to ask for partial custody, the secretary says.

Narrator, stunned and outraged, tells secretary to get out.

VIII. How This Unanticipated Result Causes Narrator to See Where and Why She Was Wrong

This is your theme! This is the moral of your story — the ideal that your story is going to prove. *This is the lesson that your narrator learns the hard way!*

Here's how it works with the narrator in our plot: Alone with this startling new development and the secretary's words whirling around in her mind, she is forced to see how things really were. For the first time, she is looking at it from her husband's viewpoint. And she sees how blindly and thoughtlessly she gave herself to the baby, leaving her husband out in the cold and consequently depriving her child of his father's affection. She realizes that she should have understood and made an extra effort to *share* the baby with him, instead of resenting his attitude and monopolizing the baby, thereby creating a barrier between father and child. Theme is realized: A woman's first duty is to her husband. It is up to them both to share their *mutual* duty to their child.

IX. NARRATOR'S REMORSE AND HER ATTEMPT TO MAKE RESTITUTION

Now your narrator tries to undo her wrong. At this point, her own affairs usually seem completely hopeless. It seems as though she has lost everything. She knows now how wrong she was, how much to blame for everything, but it seems to her that she has learned it too late!

But — because she is a better person now than she was at the beginning of the story — she is so sorry for the trouble or unhappiness she has caused that she wants to undo her mistakes (to whatever extent they can be undone), even though she expects nothing for herself.

In our plot, our narrator would want to make it up to her husband. She would face the fact that the secretary has taken good care of the child. And she would face the fact that the child needs two parents. Maybe she would decide to give up the child altogether. Or maybe she would decide to share the child equally with her husband. Whatever she decides, however, it involves a sacrifice on her part and a lot of remorse.

X. HOW NARRATOR'S REMORSE AND ATTEMPT TO MAKE RESTITUTION UNEXPECTEDLY BRING HER HAPPINESS, AFTER ALL

In almost any plot, it will pay you to find a way out of all the trouble your narrator has wrought and give her happiness. Because now that she is a much better person and willing to undo her wrong even at a sacrifice to herself, your reader will want her to be rewarded.

In our plot it is easy and natural. When the husband arrives to discuss his paternal rights in their pending divorce action, he is amazed at the change in her.

She tells him she was to blame from the beginning. And she tells him she sees this now. She tells him all the things she has realized in Element VIII. And she even humbles herself by saying she's sure the secretary will be a good stepmother to the child.

But of course we know — and the reader has surmised — that the secretary was only a stop-gap, as far as he was concerned. (And the reader isn't going to care if the secretary loses out. Any secretary who is so willing to go along in the breaking up of a marriage isn't too sympathetic a character.) Naturally the husband suggests that they try again. And, of course, the narrator resolves that this time it will be different.

And the reader is satisfied because she, too, knows that it is going to work out fine now for these two people and their child who have all become so real and important to her.

CHAPTER III

PLOTTING

The ten elements that go into the making of a typical confession story cannot be equally strong in each story; but each element must be represented even to a slight degree, or your story may not quite add up or be satisfying. On the other hand, if each element is equally strong, you'll probably end up with a novel. Usually, therefore, one or two elements are stressed, while the others are only slightly touched upon. This is *plot balance.* Your particular plot idea will determine which one or two elements are going to dominate that particular story — just as it will help you decide your best opening place and the order in which you will use the elements in writing that particular story.

But more about this later. I want to point out here that you actually have two stories in each confession. There is the immediate surface story, and the old, unsolved, underlying story. The underlying story is the past that is causing — either directly or indirectly — the present trouble, and this is the active, immediate story. In the end, both stories are solved simultaneously. The pattern, the developing of the ten elements, automatically takes care of this, as it will take care of the entire mechanical plot.

The type of problem or background that determines the character or individuality of your plot will largely depend on your own individuality — your background, your environment, your tastes, your philosophy, your experiences, and so forth. There are slight variations among different confession magazines concerning their interest in stories of teenage problems, marriage problems, family conflicts and their emphasis on and demand for the more sensational, sordid, or even criminal type of story. These preferences are due in part to the particular slant of the magazine, but these will also depend on the current needs of that magazine.

A timely subject is always good — something currently in the headlines, for example, like a sensational or unusual murder case. But here you have to be careful. You have to figure on the time it's going to take you to allow for the possibility of several rejections and possibly some rewrite work before your story sells. And then you have to take into consideration the fact that it will be months more before the story is published — by which time the subject may be out of date. For obvious reasons, then, the beginner is wise to leave this type of idea for the experienced writer who will get to the editor first.

As for the male viewpoint — approximately one fifth of the confession stories are narrated by men. If you are a man who doesn't want to write from the feminine viewpoint (although many men do!), or if for any other reason you prefer to write from the point of view of a male narrator (and many women do that because it makes a nice change of pace), don't be discouraged because I consistently use the feminine gender in my examples. To avoid the confusion of switching back and forth I have simply chosen the more popular viewpoint.

The most important thing to remember in gathering plot material for confession stories is REALISM with the semblance of REALITY. Realism is, of course, the prime requisite of the confessions. It means choosing problems and situations and solutions that are down to earth and true to life — and keeping current with the times. It means a sincere approach on your part: *You*, as author, must believe that the majority of people *want* to do the right thing, that there *is* always hope, and that there *is* some good in all of us, despite our "mistaken attitudes" and "wrong actions." The story ideas you will see all around you in life will be subconsciously seen and understood by you in terms of your own attitude toward your fellow men.

Because your aim is to write a story that represents life, the ideas that go into the making of this story must come from life as it actually is. But since it is also your aim to write a story with the unity, suspense, and significance that make good reading, you will often have to discard many of the detours and inconsistencies that exist in this actual, true story and substitute other angles to make your finished story *seem* more real than the actual story. But the *heart* of your story (that intangible quality which makes it come alive in a way a straight case history does not) depends on your own conviction, and it is therefore a big advantage to take your *starting idea* from an incident that you have, in one sense or another, personally witnessed — not ten years ago, but last week!

Another advantage in *starting* with an idea that has come

from your own experience is that your problems and situations cannot help but be real and current ones. Your character flaws will be those that actually are causing peoples' troubles, and your themes (the lessons learned) will be most apt to be universally helpful. I say your "starting" idea — you will find when you begin working with this pattern that the other elements will also come (but less deliberately) from things you have heard or seen or experienced. For all these elements are all around you every day of your life. You don't see them as *stories* because they don't come to you all fitted together into ready-made plots, with all the neatness, logic, unity, and significance a story must have. But you will learn to catalogue these various real-life incidents and problems and climaxes and flaws. Piecing them together to form one complete story will become so habitual, you will always have more plots than you can write. I will show you in a later chapter how this piecing together from one's own everyday experiences works for me. At this point, I want to show you how to spot these familiar elements and see them for what they are — vital pieces of stories.

Maybe yesterday you met someone who is so excessively envious of everyone she knows that you can't help but wonder how she got that way and how much longer her marriage can last if she keeps on making such discontented remarks in front of her husband. *You will recognize this as Element I* (CHARACTER FLAW). Or maybe some item you read in the newspaper has started you thinking — for example, the story of a young girl whose father killed her mother, then himself. This girl's face, staring at you from under the shocking headline, looks so defiant and *bitter* for a young girl just beginning her life! What is a past like this going to do to her future, you wonder. *You will see this as an idea for an El-ement II in a story.* Or maybe one of your neighbors is faced with a problem, although it's easy to see what she should do. But you know she won't handle it the right way because she has this funny quirk. And you can't tell her or she would never speak to you again. *Here you will recognize a future Element III for a plot.*

Or maybe there was a big fire in your neighborhood, and you overheard one of the firemen saying that some woman had fallen asleep with a burning cigarette. And there's a lot of whispered gossip about her having been drunk. Now you are remembering the time you accidentally found this woman in tears — and the rumor that her husband had left her for another, younger woman. Your thoughts turn to this man — the dead woman's ex-husband. *Some climax, you think!* (Element VII). What *is* going to happen now?

Or maybe while you were grabbing a bite in a coffee shop you overheard an interesting conversation in the next booth, with one woman saying heatedly, "But if I keep Timmy in his own fenced-in yard, those big bullies can't hurt him." Sensing a theme, you instinctively strained to hear more. Then you heard an older woman's calmer, gently reproving voice. "But don't forget that a fence keeps *good* things *out*." And suddenly, excitedly you know you've got a *theme* (Element VIII).

The important thing is to recognize the real-life incident in terms of the elements. It doesn't matter which one starts you off — just so you fit it into its proper place in the pattern. Then you go on from there, filling in facts for each of the other elements. But don't *try* to make two or more actual experiences fit together. It is your first idea that has intrigued you and "sparked" your story. Now you should forget your backlog of true facts and go on from there, with an eye only to filling in around this already-filled-in-element answers for each of the other elements, adding and discarding and changing until you have a neat, concise, plausible, *closely related* pattern. When you are finished, you will find that all of them have been taken from life — *but not all from one person's life.*

CHAPTER IV

CHARACTERIZATION

People read stories in general because they are interested in the *people*. The colorful or interesting background, the suspenseful plot, and the clever theme or twist are not worth anything at all if your reader isn't interested in the people who inhabit this background, who motivate or experience this plot action, or who prove out this theme.

People read confession stories in particular because they find reader-identification in them, because they can identify themselves or members of their families or their friends or enemies or acquaintances with the people in the story. When a reader says, "Why, that's just the way Cousin Jane felt when her husband left her," or "If Mrs. Thompson, next door, could read this woman's story, she would know how to keep her daughter out of trouble," etc., she is seeing herself (or those close to her) reflected in the people in your story. In other words, your characters have become real and understandable to her.

I believe characterization is the most important single quality in a story. Good characterization can carry a weak plot, while poor characterization will kill a story that evolved from a good strong plot. But failure to achieve real and understandable characters seems to be the most common single fault in beginners' stories.

Here again, reality must be the keynote. Choose characters for your plot from people you know. Give them common names for *that* person's generation. For instance, unless you have a reason, choosing a name such as Sarah or Josephine or Emma for your three-year-old girl character wouldn't carry as convincing a picture as if you named her Lisa or Kimberly or Tammy. Names have a way of going in cycles. My own name is an example of this. Many, many of my contemporaries are named *Dorothy*. But nowadays you rarely hear of a baby being named *Dorothy*. This is one small way of adding to the realness of your people, because the name you have chosen for a specific character will seem right for that character and will automatically help you to give your reader the *right* picture and that very necessary feeling of *knowing* that character.

Tell your story in the words and expressions that best suit your narrator. For instance, if your narrator is a teen-age girl, she won't tell the story of her experience in the words of an elderly college professor. Or if your narrator is a truck driver, he won't use the same words or have the same reactions that you put into the story you wrote last month that was narrated by a young mother. Consider your readers and put your characters in as nearly the same kind of environment as that of your readers as you can. For instance, if your male character has to be a big executive in a big company because it is important to your plot, you have no choice. But if the kind of job he has isn't important to the plot, let him be something farther down on the economic scale.

The majority of readers are not executives or artists or heiresses or world travelers. As we said before, a lot of them are waitresses, store clerks, factory workers, high school girls who want marriage now instead of college or a career, and housewives who do their own housework and are not in the top social or cultural drawers. If your characters need to be in environments unfamiliar to the average reader because of the nature of your plot, be sure their problems and lessons are easily applicable to your readers' lives. But if your plot can just as easily be built around people on lower economic levels, then do so, as your story will have just that much more reader-identification.

Be sure *you* are very thoroughly acquainted with *all* of your characters, even the ones who play minor roles in your story. Too often, after the beginner has learned how to plot and how to create an understandable narrator, his story fails because he has not given enough thought to his other characters. He shoves in this minor character or that one because he needs him for some specific purpose in the plot. He gives this character a name and a sex and, of course, the purpose that has brought him into the plot. And he lets it go at that. He hasn't given any further thought to this character — to what he looks like, where or how he lives, his background, etc. — and, as a result, the character has all the life and conviction of a puppet moved around a stage on a string. It doesn't matter that only three paragraphs in the entire story are devoted to this character, nor does it matter that the author knows in advance he isn't going to use any of these details about this character. *If your narrator's story is to seem real, all the people who influence her actions and reactions must seem real.*

If characterization has been your stumbling block, take the time and trouble (*after* you have worked out the details of your plot) to write your story, very briefly, from the viewpoint of each one of the characters. This will pay off in many ways. One, you will discover in this process many little inconsistencies that, if not caught and fixed, would destroy the credibility of the character and, as a result, the story as a whole. Two, you will know, when you are ready to write it from the viewpoint of the narrator, exactly how all the supporting characters should talk and act and react. Even though your narrator can express only her own thoughts, the thoughts of the other characters can be clearly implied if *you* know them. Three, without any conscious effort on your part the words you devote to each character will accomplish so much more in effect, because you will be subconsciously *implying* many more of the facts about this character than you realize. In other words, how thoroughly you know each character will determine how full-bodied, human, individual, and understandable he will come through in your story.

Your people must *act* and *react* in complete harmony with their characters and experiences as you have created them.

Many, many beginners establish a character in a certain way and then destroy the entire effect they have built by having this character speak or act or react in ways that are completely inconsistent with the reader's already formed picture of this character.

You have to go through your plot when you think you are finished, asking yourself questions: Would he say it like this? Would she feel this way? Would he do this thing? And if the action or reaction that the plot requires does not seem quite the logical action or reaction for that particular character under the particular circumstances you have created, then you must go back and *fix* it by planting or motivating or qualifying what you already have established that is causing the present discrepancy. And, remember, I am talking about *all* of the characters in your story — not *only* the narrator. If you are honest and conscientious with your story people, they will ring true and come alive for the reader.

Give your characters (and your reader) a reason for everything he says or does or thinks or feels that is not in harmony with his character as you have established it up to that point.

I have taken some examples from beginners' stories to illustrate this most common and serious of all failures . . .

In the underlying story (Element II) of one writer's failure the narrator was a girl who had loved too well and too unwisely. Then she got pregnant, her lover disappeared. This girl's upbringing was established in such a way that we could believe and understand her being so naive she could believe this heel's lies, even though the experienced reader was suspicious of his intentions . . . So far, so good! Now a messy, difficult, unhappy period follows, with the baby dying — in a logical way. Now, in the current story (that begins with Element III) this narrator meets Mr. Nice (a serviceman) who wants to marry her. But — for purposes of her intricate plot, which necessitated this narrator's getting pregnant again, unmarried, with the baby's father (Mr. Nice) unable to marry her — the writer had this narrator refuse to marry him, though she was wildly in love with him, and instead, insist on an affair. So the plot mechanism was intact.

The father of the baby was killed in the war, and the narrator was in the same predicament she was in before. But while it was understandable before, this time it was illogical. *Why* wouldn't she want marriage, I asked the author. Why would *this* girl, of all girls, with her former experience, *prefer* an affair? "Because she has to," the writer insisted, "to make the plot come out the way I want it to." Well, this wasn't a good enough reason, even though she insisted it was. The story was rejected several times, as "unconvincing," and retired . . . It could have been saved if she'd faced the character discrepancy and then set about figuring out a *believable* reason for the narrator to refuse to marry the nice fellow she loved, insisting, instead, on an affair.

Although there are always various possibilities when you start thinking, one possible way would have been to have them have a wedding date set. Then they "take" their love ahead of time — because they love each other so much and it doesn't seem wrong when they are going to be married in a week, and, besides all this, the circumstances that night "it happens" are so irresistible. And now it's easy! He is killed in an accident before the wedding, and six weeks later she knows she's pregnant — ironically, *but understandably,* in the same predicament as before.

Another beginner wrote a story that could have been pretty good if it hadn't fallen apart because of a series of small character inconsistencies. One typical example was in giving his narrator a beloved aunt who made many sacrifices, including her own financial security, in order to take proper care of this orphaned niece, the narrator. Then in the course of events, after we got to know and like this aunt, the narrator married and moved away. The story from here on covered many months' time. Yet the aunt was never even mentioned again. One wondered what had become of the aunt. There was nothing in the story that could explain how or why the girl would *forget* the existence of an aunt she had loved and to whom she had been extremely close. As a result, the narrator was neither sympathetic nor real. As it turned out, the author was through with the aunt, as far as his plot was concerned, so he didn't waste any more words on her. He didn't know why his story failed, because he didn't trouble to go through it, asking a lot of questions about his characters, the most obvious of which would have been: What about the aunt? Why wouldn't the narrator hear from her or feel obligated or grateful — or *something*? As I read this story, I wondered if the aunt had died and I had missed that sentence or paragraph. So I thumbed back, hunting for some hint of the aunt's mysterious disappearance, but found none. To the author, the aunt was never a real person, but only a puppet, dragged onto the stage for a mechanical purpose and then completely overlooked *in a way no one in life can be overlooked.*

Still another beginner wrote a story wherein the narrator's sister wanted to have a blind date with a man she had seen who was a friend of the narrator's old boy friend. The narrator is now engaged to another man, with whom she is deeply in love and very happy. But she accepts a date with the old boy friend in order to arrange a double date to include her sister and this man the sister wants to meet. She lies to her fiance, not wanting him to know that she is going on this date with her old boy friend. I won't go into the rest of the plot mechanics, but it all could have worked out IF the author had taken more time and trouble to make her characters behave convincingly. As it was, there was no convincing reason for the narrator's jeopardizing her whole future (as she knew she was doing) in order to satisfy her sister's desire to meet a certain man. One wondered why she had to date the old boy friend — why she couldn't instead merely ask him to arrange a meeting between his friend and her sister. No reason was given for ignoring this obvious and simple solution. Throughout the entire story, one had no idea what the old boy friend wanted or how he felt toward the narrator or anything else about him. And again one wondered why it wouldn't have been simpler all around if the narrator had told her fiance what she was going to do and explained why, because it would seem as though she would have been taking less risk this way. If the author had asked herself these questions when she read over her story — or better, her plot — she would have found these discrepancies and could have fixed them with very little trouble. She could have given the narrator's sister a past that included being cruelly jilted and that left her heartbroken. Then this heartbreak should have been built up and exaggerated to show that the narrator could be justifiably concerned over her sister's condition — her apathy, lack of interest in men. And when she does finally show a sign of interest in another man, the narrator could *logically* feel it is vitally important that she encourage her sister, do everything she can to bring about this meeting between her sister and this man.

If for reasons of the plot it is necessary for the narrator to lie to her fiance, the author would have to build that up in the same way. She can't simply make her fiance so unreasonably jealous she couldn't explain the situation to him, because that would make him too unsympathetic a character. But the author could invent a convincing reason for his inability to understand this situation. Perhaps he and the narrator's old boy friend were bitter enemies. If this were convincingly developed, then the narrator's decision to lie to him would be understandable. Then she would be acting and reacting in a convincing manner.

Lastly, there is the old boy friend to think about. This would be the simplest inconsistency to fix, because he doesn't have to be a sympathetic character. He can be a heel, who would probably take advantage of the narrator's situation (with regard to her sister) in order to "get even" with her fiance (his enemy). Undoubtedly, he would TELL the narrator that he will fix things between his friend and her sister IF she will give him one more date, and he would probably say that her fiance needn't ever know, intending all the time to see to it that the fiance did find out afterwards.

If all these motives had been woven into the plot, these otherwise illogical actions and reactions on the parts of all these characters would have become the *logical* actions and reactions under the circumstances.

To achieve authentic emotion, it is always better to exaggerate the *reason* for a character's hate, devotion, jealousy, envy, etc., than to exaggerate the *emotion*. For instance, the average, typical teen-age girl doesn't go into terrible agonies of heartbreak and tears over the marriage of a man she has admired from afar but has never known. The reader won't understand her heartbreak and, consequently, won't sympathize with her grief or care what happens to her. *The girl won't be real!* But, if for reasons of your plot it is necessary for this girl to react in this way, then you must give her a reason for this otherwise phony reaction that will convince the reader that *this* girl *under these particular circumstances* would react this way.

Be painstakingly careful, giving lots of critical attention to detail, get thoroughly acquainted with all your characters, and don't be so preoccupied with the plot mechanics you forget that the actions are meaningless if the reactions are not authentic!

Chapter V

PLANTING

One of the things I've never been able to understand is the constant warning against coincidence. It seems to me that coincidence is the very substance of fiction. Without it you wouldn't have a story. The secret of achieving credibility isn't in avoiding coincidence. It's in careful *planting*. It's you, as the creator of this experience, anticipating any event in your plot that is going to seem too pat (too arranged or contrived or convenient) to sound plausible to the reader. You anticipate any such possible objection by arranging your material in advance (*you are paving the way*) so that your coincidence *seems* logical.

Isn't it a coincidence when the heroine's father goes bankrupt the day before she is to marry the fortune-hunter? This convenient coincidence shows up the heel for what he is, and the girl is saved just in the nick of time. But if you read this story in a magazine, it wouldn't strike you as a coincidence. You would have been prepared ahead of time. The author would have paved the way for this coincidence by showing you how precarious the father's affairs were. You might have been told of his pressing obligations, of his strain and preoccupation in his business. You might have met the father's business partner and seen the father's suspicion of this man. All these plants would have been cleverly veiled under the immediate action which was absorbing most of your attention. When the father did go broke you might have been surprised, but you accept it as a logical turn of events. Because suddenly you were remembering these hints that hadn't seemed significant to you when you were reading them.

Let's look at an exaggerated example of this! Let's take the case of a faithless wife who has a date with the man she really loves. At the last minute the sitter can't come. She either has to leave her baby, whom she adores, alone in the house or stand up her boy friend. Now she loves this baby, but she decides to risk its safety for an hour or so in order to keep her date. Let's say that you, as the creator of this situation, are going to climax the whole thing by having the house catch on fire in the narrator's absence . . .

Now let's see how many coincidences you have here that you are going to have to prepare the reader for:

1. The sitter not being able to come . . .

Way, way back in your story you are going to begin to pave the way for this. You are going to make it clear to the reader that the sitter has a regular weekly job with the narrator. She comes automatically every Wednesday afternoon while the narrator keeps her rendezvous with the man she loves.

You are going to show that the sitter is the minister's daughter, and she has a very rigid code of morals.

You are going to show that the narrator, knowing the

sitter would be shocked if she knew the real reason for the narrator's Wednesday absences, has invented a lie to account to the sitter for these absences.

And you are going to show that the Wednesday before this present one the narrator had a bad moment when she saw the sitter's mother (same type as sitter) downtown. She was in the company of this man and *not* where she had told the sitter she was going to be. So all week she has worried because she wasn't sure whether or not the sitter's mother had seen her, too. But as time went by and nothing happened, she decided she hadn't been seen, after all.

But the mother must have seen her, because when the narrator phoned the sitter to see if she could come a little earlier than usual, the sitter coldly replied that she wasn't planning to come at all today — or any other day.

So now it isn't going to seem like a convenient coincidence to the reader. It's just an irritating complication for the narrator, but a logical one under the circumstances.

2. If this woman has been seeing this man every Wednesday and if her baby is so important to her, why, the reader will object, is it so important that she see him *this* Wednesday? Why can't she simply explain the facts to this man?

Well, why *is* it such a vital decision? How can we put more urgency into the narrator's problem — and therefore more conviction into her decision?

Let's make *this* time the narrator's *last* date with her true love. Let's say this man is going away somewhere for a long time. Maybe it's a new job or a transfer, which he grabbed at because of his hopeless situation with the narrator, which is frustrating and apparently without solution. And he and the narrator, who are fundamentally nice people who want to do the right thing, have agreed that their affair must stop!

So let's say that he is leaving today, driving with some fellow-workers who are also being transferred to this new territory. (These other fellows wanted to leave earlier, but, knowing she'd be free Wednesday afternoon, as usual, he was going to try to persuade them to leave later so he could have one more afternoon with her. And, in order to be sure, he suggested she get the baby sitter earlier, which explains how she happened to call the girl.)

So now it is a vital decision! It's her last chance to see him — maybe forever. This is their good-by!

3. Now what about this fire? How convenient, any reader would snort, that there should suddenly be a fire at this particular time and under these particular circumstances and in this particular house!

It *could* happen that way in life! But you can't get away with it in a story! So you have to plant again.

In this story perhaps you would show your narrator upstairs in the nursery with the sleeping baby, making sure the blanket couldn't slide up to smother it, making sure everything was all right, assuring herself that nothing could possibly happen. Then you would have to show her turn her thoughts from the baby back to herself, checking her time. She has one hour to get ready.

You would have to show her going into the kitchen and carefully pressing her one good dress, planning on utilizing the next hour to look her best for this last minute impression which he would take with him. You would show her noticing the spot on the skirt of the dress and hurrying to get the little bottle of naphtha she kept in the pantry, setting it down on the ironing board, dabbing at the spot — while you, as author, take the spotlight off these plants by having her harassed thoughts of this man and her hopeless situation with her impossible husband dominate the action of the scene. You are justifying the narrator's stupidity and building up the suspense. Then the phone rings. She rushes into the front hall to answer it. It's the boyfriend telling her the fellows insist on leaving in an hour. (Note: I have already paved the way for this coincidence!) He tells her he's down at the corner now, and they could have a few minutes together — if she can get away. Can't she get down there — quick? Just for a few minutes? And you show her nervousness, her emotional confusion, her need for haste. She's completely forgotten what she's going to wear and how she's going to look. All that matters is her need to see him, to have this one last moment with him. She rushes out.

Naturally there's going to be a fire!

What could be more logical — under the circumstances?

All this harks back to the popular saying that life is stranger than fiction. It isn't! In life the coincidences are accidental and they appear accidental. Because no one can anticipate them, and because no one plants (or paves the way) in advance for them . . .

In fiction the coincidences are *plotted* and they appear *plausible*. Because you, as the creator of them, know they're coming and make it your business to pave the way!

Of course you realize that the sample plot, which I used above to show you how to get around coincidences, is overloaded and much too breathless and packed to make a good story. It applies to what I said in Chapter III about Plot Balance. This story is not well *balanced* because, by the time I included the powerful motivation such a plot would require in order to keep the narrator sympathetic and convincing and a solution that would be satisfying all the way around, I would have stressed each of the elements instead of only one or two. This in itself would overburden the story even if I didn't have the added weight of the wealth of plants needed to pave the way for so many coincidences.

Don't be afraid of coincidences — but use them as sparingly as possible!

Generally speaking, most beginners learn how to take care of their big coincidences without too much trouble. What they don't seem to understand so readily is the importance of *planting* for the more routine occurrences that go into the making of every plot. Finding reasons — simple, logical, plausible reasons — for the various things your characters do and for the things that happen to these characters and giving these reasons to your reader becomes an automatic habit when you understand that this type of planting makes all the difference between a seemingly contrived story and a seemingly inevitable experience.

I'm not talking about character inconsistency now, but

merely the various ways in which you must move your characters around to conform with the mechanics of your plot.

For instance, it is perfectly natural for a woman to drop
in at a friend's house unexpectedly, isn't it? If these two
women are old friends and if they live close by and if they
are more or less free for visiting in the afternoons, it becomes even more natural, doesn't it? Now, if this old friend's
husband is secretly seeing the narrator, *this time* at the narrator's home, it *could* very easily be that his wife would
happen to drop in on her friend at *that time*. But because it
is *too convenient* for your plot to have this happen in just
this way, your story will seem contrived and, therefore,
unreal.

However, if you showed earlier, within a scene that was
dominated by a different, stronger, more immediate angle
(i.e., if you *slipped it in* unobtrusively) that this old friend
had borrowed something the narrator needed and had failed
to return it yesterday, as she planned, then it becomes
inevitable that she would drop in *today*.

Another example of the need for this type of planting is
when the weather plays a part in the plot action. Anyone
can be caught in a rainstorm. There is nothing unusual or
illogical about that. But when the narrator, who is an inex-
perienced driver, is rushing to the hospital on an emergency
and gets caught in the rain, which causes her to have an
accident, then the rainstorm has become too convenient
for purposes of your plot. All the author would have to do
would be to slip in a sentence or two earlier, *unobtrusively*
letting the reader know that it was the rainy season or that
it was a dark, gloomy day or that it had been an unseason-
ably dry season and the farmers were praying for a long

overdue rainfall — any such casual remark that will *pave the way* for the rain that is going to play a part in your plot action.

Once again it's a case of going through your plot and searching for all the places where a reader could wonder *why*. If the answer isn't obviously apparent, then you had better figure one out and slip it in.

Why did the store deliver the wrong dress, causing the narrator to go to the big, important party in an old, unattractive dress, thereby ruining her self-confidence, which in turn made it impossible for her to compete with her rival? (Show the stupidity of the clerk when the narrator bought the dress.) *Why* did the narrator's cake fail the night she was entertaining her husband's boss? (Show earlier, when she was preparing the dinner, that she was trying a new, unfamiliar recipe — or that she found it necessary to substitute for a certain ingredient.)

In life these everyday occurrences do come about without any reason at all, and they have a way of happening when it is least convenient. But if they happen this way in your story, without any *specific* reason, your story will not ring true. It will be too obvious to the reader that the author arranged everything to fit his plot. Making everything *seem* inevitable adds only a sentence or two to your story, but it makes a big difference in credibility.

CHAPTER VI

BUILDING A STORY

I want to convince you that my system really does work, and I want to show you how much fun it is. So I'm going to take you through all the steps with me.

First, I need an idea to get me started, so I thumb through my notebook marked IDEAS. This is where I jot down reminders whenever something strikes me as a story germ. And I see a notation, *June — Saw R.H. coming out of a nightclub with a young woman.* And then I remember that night . . .

How shocked I'd been to see Roger Harris — that isn't his name, but it will do here — gazing adoringly down into the seductive little face of a girl who was young enough to have been his daughter. He and his wife were neighbors, and I'd been glad he hadn't seen me. I'd scurried away, thinking about his wife, wondering if she knew. I'll call her Kate. I decided she didn't. Because I'd seen her in the supermarket the day before, and she'd shown me pictures of her new grandson. She'd sounded proud and happy — with none of the droop of a betrayed wife! No, Kate hadn't known then. But she must have found out shortly after that, when Roger had moved out and she'd started her suit for divorce. Now their house was sold, and we'd all lost track of them. I kept thinking about it, with one part of my mind sadly remembering and the other part groping for a plot. Their marriage failure was sad, but not surprising. Kate was too old-fashioned, too reluctant to move with the times. Her house had been filled with antiques, and her clothes — that she made herself — always had the look of a decade ago. I remembered how she'd pursed her lips when one of our mutual friends had got a new combination washer-dryer, how self-righteously superior she'd sounded when she'd said, "But laundry smells so much cleaner when it's dried outdoors." The other gal and I had smiled at each other, not arguing. Kate was one of those if-it-was-good-enough-for-my-mother before-me-it's-good-enough-for-me types. She'd wanted life to stand still. And Roger hadn't. It was that simple!

I thought about it a while, feeling sorry for her and finally realizing I still wasn't getting a story out of it. Besides, *today's* confession market isn't eager for middle-aged narrators.

So I began thumbing through my notes and clippings again, remembering and discarding and trying not to feel discouraged. And then I found another one that sparked my interest. It was a small newspaper item about the suicide of a girl I'll call Linda. She'd been identified as a sixteen-year-old runaway, who'd been missing a year at the time of her death. The article disclosed the fact that she was pregnant. And sick. And unmarried. I'd clipped it out of the paper because it was the kind of thing good stories are made of!

And maybe this is the time to make that story, I think,

as I try to imagine what this girl was all about. Why did she run away from home? I can easily imagine the terrible experiences she must have had . . . And her disillusion and despair — and the awful fear when she found she was pregnant. What did she learn from her mistakes and suffering, I wonder.

But of course I can't let her kill herself — not if she's going to be my next narrator, with a lesson to learn that's going to brighten her future, not snuff it out.

I start digging around in my imagination for a suitable background for her, one that will *logically* drive her away from home. I can think of dozens, of course, but the trouble is I don't want it to be so bad she can't *logically*, after she learns her lesson, return to it.

And then it hits me! What if she has a mother like Kate Harris — a mother who clings to the past the way Kate did? The teens are a rebellious period anyway, and this way *this* girl will have more than usual justification for rebelling against a mother like this.

Suddenly I feel the excitement of knowing I have a plot now, with people who are real to me. But the pieces are coming too fast, and I know from past experience how elusive they are and that I must get them written down before they slip away from me.

So I take ten sheets of paper, heading each one up with one of the TEN ELEMENTS. I know from experience that I'm going to keep going from one to another and back again, adding and deleting and changing as new ideas and details develop — because I also know from experience that it pays to be very sure that each bit of information gets into its proper element.

Then I start going through these papers, filling in what I already have:

ELEMENT I — Rebelliousness; immature values.

ELEMENT II — I will make her the only child of Kate and Roger, whom I'm going to take verbatim from the "Kate" and "Roger" I used to know. So this element, this time, is going to be easy. Kate puts too much stock in tradition, antiques, roots; she clings to the old, automatically condemning anything modern — because it's new. She indulges in polite white lies and small, kind, face-saving hypocrisies. Thus, she and Linda are in constant conflict, with Linda, a typical, modern, adventuresome young girl, attracted to the new and different.

I think about Linda, my narrator. Since this is *her* story — since, in a sense, *I* am going to be *Linda*, I'm going to have to know all the details of her experience, and I see no advantage in having her run away. Why not have her meet her future "lover" in the normal course of events?

So I'll have her meet a fellow who represents everything Kate deplores — who, being the antithesis of her mother, is, therefore, exciting to Linda. I have to stop and think about him. I decide to name him Gabe. I jot down a few notes to describe him. To keep my story as current as possible, I decide to have him be the perpetual college student type; he takes great pride in being poor, living like a bum, looking sloppy and unkempt. He goes out of his way to flaunt his disregard for the old and established (because this sharpens the conflict between him and Kate). He is contemptuous of money and hypocrisy in any degree, believing in honesty to the point where he pulls no punches. He has no plan to do anything constructive, living LITERALLY for *this* day, without the slightest regard or concern for yesterday or tomorrow. If I make him good-looking and persuasive, I think a boy like this could logically be attractive to a frustrated girl like Linda.

So she falls in love with him, and, since it would be completely out of HIS character to marry her, she will have to have an affair with him. But she's my narrator, and I want her to be sympathetic in spite of her rebelliousness — and, therefore, I want her to be basically a *nice* girl, who holds out for marriage.

That's the way I *want* her to be, but, in all honesty, I'm not convinced that this girl, under the circumstances I've so far established, would be like this. So I need another reason, and finally I remember Roger, who is going to be her father. I remember that he's more moderate, and now I realize it would be logical that this girl would feel extra close to him, with him often serving as the buffer between her and Kate. I think Linda is aware of his unhappiness with Kate's stubborn clinging to the past and her unreasonable rejection of the new, which causes her to be more defensively loyal to her father, more anxious to please him — and more critical of her mother.

ELEMENT III — So it is her love for her father, her desire not to disappoint or hurt him, that motivates her refusal to give in to Gabe's very persuasive pleas for sex, which she wants desperately — but with marriage! This is her problem.

But how does she meet him? I decide she's a freshman

in college, living at home. And now I know this story has to be set in a university town — with Gabe's family far away somewhere.

ELEMENT IV — As I said, I know marriage would be out of character for him. But she has to give in to his sexual demands in order to get pregnant — which I've already decided is my climax. So something has to happen that justifies her giving in. I can't think of anything, and I want to see what else I have — so I move ahead.

ELEMENT V — She probably HOPES that she will be able to make him so happy he will want to marry her. Also, she will naturally hope for the joy of fulfilling her love — i.e., sex!

ELEMENT VI — This is the body of my story; it's the affair in action, showing her lies, deceits, THRILLS (my sex scenes), worries, sneaking, meanwhile despising her mother, who is living in a cocoon, she thinks, and — !

Her Father! Now it dawns on me that her discovery of her father's "other woman" is my perfect MOTIVATION for her sudden willingness to enter into the affair she has been fighting. Because this discovery would shock and hurt and disillusion her, and she can logically and understandably and sympathetically figure that if *he* can do it, why shouldn't *she*? So I add all this onto my

ELEMENT IV sheet.
Now I'm moving on to finish up with

ELEMENT VI — In here I will show how Gabe's honesty

she'd once admired is becoming ugly and cruel to her. And I have to pave the way for her pregnancy. But in this day and age, with intelligent, informed people like Linda and Gabe, it has to be an accident that happens IN SPITE OF THEIR PRECAUTIONS. But I don't want to get hung up on this technical (though important) point now. What I will do is phone a friend of mine who is a receptionist for a group of doctors, including a gynecologist. I'll take her to lunch and ask her how this could *logically* happen to this *enlightened* young couple. If she doesn't know, she'll find out for me, and I'll thank her with a gift. This is the way I do most of my "research." But, thinking about this, I decide that — for this period of time — the pill would be the way they've been preventing it. Anyway, whatever it is that does go wrong that ultimately is going to cause her unwanted pregnancy HAS TO BE PLANTED HERE.

ELEMENT VII — The climax begins when she discovers, to her absolute horror, that she is pregnant. She tells Gabe, hoping and praying that he will surely realize he has to marry her now. Gabe not only flatly refuses, but he insists that she let a med student friend of his perform an abortion. "He owes me a favor," Gabe says. Horrified, she refuses. (Because *right now* the favorable consideration of an abortion is not too acceptable for a confession narrator — and too unsympathetic of her.) So she pleads with him. The end of the CLIMAX comes when he walks out on her, completely disappearing without a trace.

ELEMENT VIII — Now she has to learn her lesson. I'm not sure about this. I don't think it would be acceptable to uphold Kate's way, even if I could believe it's right. Which I don't! I try to imagine what *this* girl would think right now, under these circumstances. She would certainly think about Gabe now. And she would logically see his faults now. So this is when she sees that this has always been Gabe's way — to run away from life and its responsibilities. . . That his way is a selfish, self-indulgent, undisciplined form of escape — which he has disguised with a lot of criticism of the ones who work and assume responsibility and believe in things like duty and consideration and — yes, she thinks suddenly, *love!* Because Gabe never really loved her — he didn't know anything about love. Only *self*-love! With Gabe it was really just sex — which he called love. I still need a theme, I realize. But in the meantime, seeing him as he really is, she is freed of her infatuation for him.

ELEMENT IX — But she isn't freed of her trouble. She may consider suicide, but, even though she considers her own life ruined and futureless, she knows she couldn't go through with it because she couldn't take another, innocent life — her baby's.

So, humbled, sorry, and ashamed, she has no choice but to tell her mother, who surprisingly isn't condemning of her situation, but reassures and comforts her — and then confesses that she knows about her husband's mistress and has seen the error of *her* ways. She sees she drove them *both* away from her (her child and her husband) by not moving ahead with the times — with life — instead of trying to hold it still. And — the mother says (back to THEME)

ELEMENT VIII — that LIFE NEVER STANDS STILL. WE HAVE TO MOVE WITH IT. (But I'm still not satisfied that this is the real theme of this story that will totally tie it all together.)

ELEMENT X — I still don't have a happy ending for my story either. Gabe is out of it. But this girl deserves some hope for herself now that she has suffered and learned. And her baby is going to need a father. So why couldn't an old boyfriend — Mr. Right, though she didn't realize that before Gabe came along — come back into the picture? And it does make sense that a girl like this — with enough attractiveness to appeal to a fellow like Gabe — would have had a boyfriend before she met and fell for him, doesn't it?

So I stop here and create another character, her boyfriend before Gabe. To add this new character, I go back to

ELEMENT II — I'll name him Howie, and I'll have him represent the clean-cut type all mothers like for their daughters, especially a mother like Kate. Linda has known him a long time, and the families are friends. I shall make him as opposite from Gabe as possible — responsible, decent, dependable, faithful — but of course UNEXCITING to a girl like Linda. He, too, is in the University, planning to become a teacher. Naturally Kate is crazy about him, which puts him down even more in Linda's estimation. When Gabe comes into her life, she and Howie quarrel and break up — much to Kate's disappointment.

ELEMENT X — Now I have Howie coming gradually back

into the picture, resuming their friendship, making it obvious to the reader that something good is going to come of this because he still loves her and is a big enough man to understand and forgive and love another man's baby — and because she now, being a more mature person due to her sad experience, appreciates him in a way she didn't before.

But what about Kate and Roger? I think about them and find the solution. I'll have the narrator admit to her father that she knew about his affair, got mad, realizes now it was none of her business, and this is her apology to him for making such a mess of her life and causing him all the disappointment and shame and worry. She admits to him that she knows now she was wrong to think that what *he* did gave *her* license to do the wrong thing *she* did . . . This makes him feel guilty and ashamed, and his "other woman" no longer appeals to him. Thus, he is able to see that his wife, Kate, *is* trying to change now, and the two of them make a new start.

And now, suddenly, I have the *real* theme for this story. So I pull out that sheet again to put it down.

ELEMENT VIII — The middle road is always best, whereas an extreme in either direction causes trouble.

And now I realize that Linda's father, Roger, is the ideal character to keep planting this theme, in his own words, of course, and I reach again for my sheet for

ELEMENT II — So that I can remind myself that in this section I am going to need a couple of specific incidents in which Roger tries to settle the arguments between Kate and Linda, trying to get Kate to take a more modern view

of things, trying to get Linda to be more tolerant and appreciative of the established, homely virtues.

I'm pleased with my new plot. All the pieces are here, and
they all fit together. And now, after working with the *people,*
they have become very real to me. I know them!

I'm ready to start writing my first draft now, opening
with the problem, of course. And since sex scenes are so
salable these days, I'll open with Gabe and Linda, alone
somewhere, with Gabe wanting to make love, with Linda
wanting it, too, but holding back — holding out for marriage. In this opening scene, I'll show her desperate hints
and his arguments against marriage and for an affair. They
make sense to her, but she can't bring herself to give in.
Later, when she's at home, in bed, feeling frustrated and
discouraged and wondering how long she can hold him off,
wondering how she can get him to marry her, she can't help
but compare him with Howie, who IRONICALLY was always the one to pull away before things got out of hand,
who begged her to marry him.

This train of thought causes her to remember Howie —
and now I'm successfully *and logically* launched into my
flashback (ELEMENT II), which I'll present in a briefer,
less dramatic way than the rest of the story. In *this* story,
when I get back up to the opening point in the natural
chronology, she will still be in her depressed mood.

But a couple of nights after this she discovers her father's
two-timing, and now she is ready to make her WRONG
DECISION — ELEMENT IV.

It's going to be easy. And fun! All I have to do is follow
along, the way I follow a map on a trip.

Chapter VII

WRITING

Now you have learned how to build a plot with all the necessary ingredients, you have learned how to make all of the actions and the reactions of all your characters consistent and realistic, you have included in your plot, in the proper places, the various necessary plants, you have decided on the best opening place for your particular story — and you are ready to *write*.

Writing is, to some extent, the expression of one's personality. In the confession story it is your narrator's personality that must come through in the telling of *her* story. Some people have more natural writing fluency than others, and for everyone practice brings improvement. Still, there are rules and tricks and short-cuts that can eliminate a lot of gruelling trial and error and make the job of transforming your plot into a readable, salable story easier and quicker.

Many beginners make the mistake of dramatizing and pulling out all the factual and less interesting sections of the story and then selling the high spots short, thus failing to build the reader's suspense or to stir her emotions. Not only is the reader bored, but she is unconvinced that any of it is very important anyway.

64

The best way to avoid this is to write your story through from beginning to end in straight narration, starting, of course, with the place where you intend to open the finished draft. This is a good way of spotting the natural highlights in the story. The highlights are the episodes that should be fully developed with dialogue, gestures, and emotions so that the reader may participate right along with the narrator. The more passive, prosaic sequences, without which there could be no highlights, should be narrated in a conversational style. The author must keep in mind the fact that the narrator is confiding her innermost secrets to the reader, and the entire tone should communicate this sense of intimacy.

Use of the present tense (that is, living the story at the same time it's being written), too much dialogue and too many characters make a confession story sound fictional and tend to destroy the simple reality which is the all-important basis for a confession story. The writer must never, *never* forget that her story *has been lived* and is being revealed on paper in such a way that the readers will be stirred and can live the experience vicariously and so be helped to avoid making a similar mistake. This is the total impression that your finished story must convey.

It's not only important that you keep reading the *current* published stories, but it's just as important that you read them with the right attitude. Don't make the mistake so many beginners make by looking for and finding and exulting over all the flaws — and saying, "If they buy a terrible story like this, I can't understand why they rejected mine. It *must* be luck." But it isn't luck. And this sort of self-indulgent criticism only hurts *you,* as a selling writer. . .

Because it keeps you from finding out what there was in or about that story that the editor liked — *what made that story sell! That's* what you should be looking for when you read — because that's what's going to help you make your next story more salable.

TRANSITIONS

TRANSITIONS are difficult for some beginners. In the confessions, more so than in other types of fiction, a great span of time is often covered in a short story. In such cases it is necessary to make great jumps of time in a very few words.

I have read beginners' manuscripts that could and should have been cut in half but were so overlong because the authors did not know how to make the break between the *pertinent* episodes. So they strung these episodes together with long, unnecessary, boring passages.

The following examples of this are taken from a story about a girl who married a man she didn't love after she was jilted by the man she did love. The story shows, among other things, how and why this marriage failed.

This bit shows why she married him:

> He didn't kiss me good-night when we got home. But he was more like the Rod I knew. "Forget this night, will you, Janey?" He grinned wryly. "I'll put off my proposal till next time. But remember, I'm the guy who's going to pursue pleasure, and you're the girl who's going to help me."
>
> I said lightly, "We'll forget the other, Rod."
>
> But after he left, I didn't forget it. I thought about it all that night and finally thought I'd figured it out. Rod

had been hurt — too deeply. But all he needed was someone to be close to, to help him find a real purpose in life. Someone to help dissolve the loneliness in his heart.

And I wondered if *I* had someone, would the awful ache in mine dissolve? In a way we were in the same boat, each of us wishing things might have been different — but each of us drifting aimlessly . . .

I married Rod that April.

There were other reasons. For one, I was deathly tired of living alone, afraid of the bleak future of it. I'd been alone so long. Everything in me cried out for a different kind of life — a home, children, being a part of a family.

And even though I hadn't forgotten Pete, he *was* out of my life. I didn't see why it couldn't work out.

Those first few weeks I wasn't even aware of Rod's restlessness. But after the night of the Carter wedding I began to realize there isn't any substitute for love . . .

It was a garden affair, early that June. We . . .

Now the author goes into this episode, which is a highlight because it is a turning point in her life, the occasion that first made her realize her mistake.

In the first draft the author had a page between . . . *but each of us drifting aimlessly* and the next paragraph, *I married Rod that April,* telling all the unimportant things that happened before the marriage and another page describing the details of the wedding. None of that had any bearing on *this* story and slowed it up unnecessarily. She was able to delete those pages by making a definite statement (*We were married in April*) and following it with the two paragraphs that tell her rationalization to the reader.

In the author's plot, she used a series of specific incidents that showed how this marriage failed. But because she didn't know how to jump smoothly from one incident to another, she had pages of irrelevant and confusing and boring details in between each one. All she needed was a sentence or two *telling* the reader — *in advance of the episode* — the result of the episode. Then, after telling the reader, she *showed* the episode, so the reader could see for herself that it all was the way the narrator said it was.

Here is another section from this same story that shows how easy it is to jump from one episode to another by tucking in front of each episode a sentence or two that *tells* the purpose of the episode before *showing* it.

The narrator is rationalizing the previous episode that showed Rod's independence of her, his refusal to let her take care of him . . .

Rod didn't need a wife to "mother him." He needed only the kind who was always ready for fun . . .

I wouldn't even give up, though, when I discovered one afternoon that he didn't really need *me* for that.

He had called from the office, wanting me to come downtown for dinner, explaining that the wife of one of the fellows had a younger sister visiting from out of town. They wanted to show her the sights and wanted Rod and me to come along.

I had to stay in bed that morning, had been trying all day to throw off a cold that was threatening. "Not tonight, Rod," I begged off, explaining. "Will you pick up some aspirin on your way, dear?" I went on. It simply didn't occur to me he wouldn't be on his way home in an hour.

"I can," he said agreeably, "but why don't you phone the drug store for some? It'll be after midnight before this thing breaks up, you know."

I said yes, I'd phone. And I sat, holding the receiver long after he had hung up, trying hard to believe that there wasn't any reason why he *shouldn't* stay down without me.

But, of course, I was bound to have to face it eventually.

The bleached blond who popped in on me so dramatically one afternoon in August made it all so perfectly clear even I couldn't pretend any longer.

I took her all in in one second — her coarse kind of made-up prettiness, her exotic perfume, her too tight knit suit — and knew exactly what she was going to say.

When you make these abrupt jumps by use of a *preview sentence,* you must remember to be specific and clear, both as to *status* and *time.*

FLASHBACK

Some beginners have difficulty in finding the right places in their stories for the FLASHBACK, and others have trouble getting into the flashback sequences smoothly and clearly and naturally and without a lot of preliminary words.

Choosing the right place for your flashback depends, to some extent, on the individual story. But if you go back from a place in the present part of your story that will leave your reader with a feeling of suspense, you will be more assured of her interest as you take her back. But while it is advisable to go back *after* you have thoroughly acquainted her with the immediate problem and situation, you must be careful to take her back *before* she becomes confused as to the facts and reasons behind this immediate problem and situation. This is automatically accomplished if you go back between Element III and Element IV.

In order to avoid an abrupt, awkward jerking back, you must see to it that the tail end of your present scene seems to lead *naturally* into the past, so that it appears to be *inevitable* for your narrator to go back. This is accomplished by ending your present scene with a thought or a speech that leads directly into the starting point of your flashback. And this lead-off sentence is usually arranged quite deliberately by the author.

An example of this is from the same story of the narrator who married one man, even though she was still in love with the man who jilted her. The author opened this story during one of the narrator's dates with the man she didn't love before she married him. Her romance with the man who jilted her is in the past. They are sitting in a nightclub in this opening scene . . .

"In no time at all, you'll even forget what the guy looked like," Rod assured me.

I wanted to believe him. I didn't argue, didn't remind him that after six months I still remembered vividly every detail of Pete's face, every intonation of his voice, every word he had said that last day . . . (and now she's back into the past scene with Pete).

Coming back to the present from a flashback is easier. All you have to do is take the reader back to the place where you left off and *make sure she knows exactly where she is in the chronology of the story.*

PLANTS

Weaving in PLANTS so that the reader is aware of them only subconsciously is one of the most mechanical aspects of writing. You, as author, know what you want to bring out earlier in the story because you know that the twist later in your story won't ring true if you haven't paved the way for it. But your narrator (and your reader) mustn't know at that earlier time that the incident (plant) is going to make the twist (climax) inevitable because you want them to be surprised; so you, as author, must *weave this plant within a more pressing, immediate issue that will logically absorb the narrator's (and the reader's) conscious attention.*

The following paragraph is from a story in which the narrator's husband has been paralyzed in an automobile accident. The operation proved unsuccessful. The claim he has put in to the insurance company of the man responsible for the accident is pending. Meanwhile, the husband is insisting on a divorce. The narrator feels, understandably, that, even though their marriage was a failure before the accident, she can't leave him now. As the story turns out, the husband was faking his injury in order to defraud the insurance company. Much, much planting for the many angles of this story was necessary. One of the many plants for the later-to-be-divulged fact that he *can* walk was worked in *under the guise* of the narrator's pity for him, thus:

I couldn't stop trying. Not even after Dick was home, moodily silent, spending most of his time behind the locked door of the guest room, insisting he was leaving, alone, as soon as the case was settled! I told myself the gnawing worry of money on top of losing the use of one's legs would make anyone unreasonable. . . . etc. . . .

UNITY

UNITY will be automatically accomplished if the elements are developed one in relation to the other, as was demonstrated in Chapter II, and if the tie between the Character Flaw and the Theme is a close one. Frequently, the Character Flaw is the *negative* attitude of the *positive* premise that is your theme. If your story seems to be wandering too far from the main issue, find the sequence that is destroying its unity. If it is something you don't need, cut it out. If you do need it, present it through your narrator's misguided viewpoint. This will bring it into closer harmony with the rest of the story.

CLARITY

CLARITY can be achieved by anticipating reader questions. Wherever a question naturally arises is where more explanation is needed. Beginners often mistake *confusion* for *suspense*. When the reader wonders breathlessly, "How can she possibly get out of this?" Or, "What is going to happen now?" you have created suspense. But when the reader wonders, "What is this all about?" Or, "Have I missed something somewhere?" then you have failed to be as clear as you must be.

Emotion

The EMOTION in your story must be genuine, and it must be powerful. The short story has accurately been defined as "a narrative with an emotional purpose." This is especially true of the confession story. The more strongly you can move your reader, the more successful your story will be. If you can make your reader cry, you've got it made. I personally think the tear-jerker type of story is more popular than any other kind — and in any period of time, i.e., the tear-jerker has a *timeless* appeal! I have already discussed in Chapter IV the ways and means of achieving authentic emotion — real, life-like characters attempting to solve real problems in ways that are understandable and sympathetic to the reader. Now I want to say something about the writing of it.

One student had so much trouble getting any emotional transference into her otherwise excellent stories that we finally came up with the idea of having her ignore the emotion while she concentrated exclusively on all the other aspects of writing her story, until she was satisfied. Then, in a completely separate operation, she was to go back through it and *deliberately* inject the emotion into each sentence, in a purely mechanical way. And what started out as a practice assignment turned out to be a very successful method — for *her!*

Other beginners seem to think that the only way to convey strong emotion is to describe it lengthily. Violent weeping, madly racing blood, pounding, hammering hearts, etc., are typical, overworked examples of this. The beginner stops the forward movement of his story completely cold — because this is *telling* the emotion, and emotion to be transmitted must be *shown*. If a reader is to *feel* the narrator's emotion, she must see it in action.

Emotion depicted through gesture, action, speech, and thought, as it is *woven in* with the telling of the story, is infinitely more *effective* and more *convincing*.

Listed below are several unrelated sentences that *show* the narrator's emotion without halting the story action:

Everyone was staring at me. I could feel it. I looked around defiantly, from face to face, and knew I'd said too much . . .

I didn't take my eyes from the sedative I was mixing, but I knew instinctively she was talking about *me* . . .

My knees felt so rubbery I had to grasp hold of the table to keep standing . . .

I cleared my throat and tugged at my bracelet . . .

I pressed past him, not answering. I hauled my coat from the closet, yanked it on, and fumbled with the buttons . . .

The receiver dropped from my hand . . .

I slumped into the last seat, wishing I had a paper to hide behind . . .

Doggedly I kept on with the wedding gifts, working with limp, white tissue paper that felt almost soggy. I merely wrapped and addressed, not bothering to enclose explanatory notes. Everyone already knew all there was to know . . .

Suddenly I had to get home. I stood up, my gloves and bag spilling off my lap onto the floor. I stepped forward and almost lost my balance, as my knees crashed into the coffee table . . .

The phone began to ring. But I didn't move. I sat, stupidly speculating on it. It could be . . .

"I hoped I'd find you home," I said, puffing from the stairs and the heat — and the thing I was going to have to say . . .

"But I can't just walk out on him." My voice came out thin past the lump in my throat.

His words didn't mean anything to me. I saw only my dreams, shattering . . .

I listened, managing to hold myself together in spite of the unnerving compassion in the old doctor's voice as he told me . . .

I forced a smile and chattered on nervously . . .

I kept my eyes grimly averted, asking stiffly, "You had something to tell me?" . . .

Those minutes seemed like years . . .

Then he picked up his case and quietly walked out — just as if he hadn't dropped a bomb right in the middle of our lives. It must have been minutes after the door clicked before Ray's voice cut through the stunned silence . . .

His voice was awfully quiet when he did speak. So was his face, as he looked steadily at me . . .

No one moved. The room and everyone in it seemed suddenly inanimate. Everything except my own thoughts, whirling back . . .

Dazed, I watched him open one of his bags, saw the contents spill over the sides. I stared at the untidiness without thinking about it. "Yes, of course I understand, dear," I murmured. But I *didn't* understand . . .

I pushed savagely on the elevator button, then swung around to face her. "I wouldn't run after any man. I wouldn't want a man I had to trap on the rebound," I flung out. It was all I could do to keep from slapping her pretty, smug, mocking face. Just in time the elevator lurched to a stop, and I jammed myself inside it . . .

My hand trembled so I had to lay the list down on the desk so it would be still enough to read . . .

I crouched at the closed door, holding my breath, picturing the police swarming over the house with their eternal probing questions. *I* might be called on for something . . .

I saw Barbara come in, an amused half-smile on her lips. Then I gasped and set my glass down with a bang. For there was Dave, beside her, with that old expression of tortured delight, holding one of her creamy-white arms as if he would never let it go. Rigid with anger and fear, I lowered my eyes and tried to squeeze back the tears. I felt and heard our table filling up again, heard the familiar voices all around me. But I couldn't look up, not until . . .

Sometimes it is helpful to make use of outer conditions,

that have nothing to do with the story or the characters, to help you set the mood for the emotion you are trying to transfer. Notice how the descriptions of the weather listed below convey in themselves the feeling of the narrator who is noticing them:

> The dark outside seemed more pearl-gray now, suddenly less leaden and oppressive . . .

> The air was heavy, suggestive of a faint odor of mildew. The street and sidewalk were empty and silent, as if the day itself were lifeless, already spent . . .

> I stared fixedly between the garage and the fence where the west horizon was barely visible. Yes, it *was* a quiet sunset tonight — no burst of color, no magic glory . . .

Consider for a moment how *your* impressions of *things* — the weather, your clothes, your reflection in the mirror, the meaningless remarks people make, the sight of your own home, standing in line, and so forth — vary with your mood. Let your narrator respond to conditions irrelevant to her immediate problem in the same way, and the emotion you wish to transfer to your reader will be that much more potent.

You must be careful, however, that you do not bring into your story unrelated and unnecessary matters for this purpose. If you did, your story would be *rambling* and as a result would lose the compactness and unity every short story must have. Use this device only where the story action makes room for it without much addition of words. For instance, if your narrator is outdoors, there *is* weather. If she is sad, make it, in a sentence, a gray, melancholy sort of day; if she is happy, let the day be bright and spring-like; if she is angry, she might be fighting her way through a raw March wind. And so on . . . This is a mechanical device for *pointing up* the emotion, not to be overdone, but to be used wherever an occasion seems ready-made for it.

BEING SPECIFIC

Be SPECIFIC about little things. Give your town a name. Give your characters *specific* jobs. If you refer to a dress, give its color. If a big scene takes place while the characters are eating dinner, then *weave in with* their actions, speech, and reactions some of the specific things they are eating. If a book is important enough in your story to be mentioned, then mention the kind of book it is. Don't *overdo* descriptions — just be specific about whatever it is you are talking about. Too many beginners refer to the various affairs that surround their narrators' lives so vaguely that the whole story has a nebulous, unreal tone, when it should come through as an actual, true-life experience. And this is one of the "little things" that helps.

DIALOGUE

DIALOGUE is one of the "big things" and the source of a lot of trouble for most beginners. One reason for this is carelessness. The author hasn't taken enough time or trouble to make sure his character is speaking as that particular character would speak. As a result, the characters all speak exactly as the author himself speaks, or, worse, they use such formal, stilted words and phraseology that they are, literally, out of this world.

Another cause for trouble, though, is not knowing the various "tricks" of making dialogue sound natural. One trick is to break off a speech now and then — as people in actual conversations frequently do — by the speaker himself, because a sudden thought has occurred to him; or because, either having made his point or feeling hopelessly unable to make it, he simply drifts off; or by another character who interrupts; or by some other kind of interruption, such as the ringing of the doorbell or telephone. The following examples illustrate some of the various ways of breaking off dialogue:

"I've heard of your kind," she said scornfully, "but I hoped if I talked to you, you'd — " She stopped and bit her lip, and I realized she couldn't be nearly so experienced as she looked . . .

"Terry has never asked for his freedom," I told her quietly. "But anytime he does . . . " What was the use? She wasn't going to believe *me* . . .

I whirled around sharply. "But he — "

"He's back — came back right after we were married," Mike put in quickly.

Long, unbroken speeches can make a story as dull as one without any dialogue. People in everyday life don't make long speeches without doing something after a sentence or two or without changing tones as their *feelings* enter into what they are saying. They pause, hesitate, repeat, interrupt themselves to make a point or a qualification or to ask a question.

Jed's voice broke into the silence. "Funny," he drawled, "that nobody asks how I know it was murder. Or did you all discover, too, that there was no trace of blood on the fireplace where somebody wanted me to think she'd fallen?" He shifted his weight and looked at Mr. Steele slowly and deliberately. "But there *were* traces of blood — recent blood — on the loose brick."

"She wasn't expecting me, but she'll be happy just the same." He grinned and stared at me as if — well, as if he were very pleasantly surprised. Even his voice was full of charm. Soft and husky and sort of intimate, saying, "As it is, it's sure a break for me Aunt Isobel *isn't* home."

"He's a nice guy, Sally." Jim climbed out and came around to open my door. Tucking my arm through his, as we started up the walk, he added, "I can't see what you have against him. I think it would be nice if — "

"It would be awful," I burst out.

"Let's not waste our time pretending," he begged softly, slipping his hand over mine. "Let's admit we know something happened to both of us the minute we saw each other." His voice dropped to a whisper. "Let's take every second we can manage together."

Dialogue should serve several purposes simultaneously. While one is hearing that character speak, one should see

him and feel with him. And at the same time the story
should continue to *move* forward. If your narrator is speaking, her thoughts are easily and naturally woven in with
her speech, as below:

> "It wasn't that way," I protested. I knew how she felt.
> This was just another rotten break for her. "I only waited
> because . . . "

Another device for breaking the monotony of a long speech
of explanation is to throw part of it into *indirect* speech; i.e.,
let the narrator report to the reader the *gist* of what the
speaker is telling her, as below:

> "I mean she's funny about me," he said carefully, "sort
> of jealous and suspicious of anybody *I* like." She had
> always been like that, he added. "I suppose having no
> son of her own — and her unhappy marriage with Stan
> — " He supposed those things made her that way. Lately
> she had been even worse, probably because of her illness.
> She was in a bad nervous state. But he humored her.
> "Seems the least I can do when she's done so much for
> me," he finished, his smile asking me to understand.

In this way the reader gets the necessary information
quickly and the impression of dialogue and immediacy
without actually getting it in too solid a lump.

Never give information to the reader through dialogue if
that information would logically be obviously known to
both the speaker and listener.

In one beginner's story it was necessary to the plot to

establish the fact that this husband and wife always had dinner at seven o'clock. To get this information over to the reader, the author worked it into the dialogue, so that the narrator said to her husband, "We always have dinner at seven."

If they always do, obviously he knows it. Therefore, how *unnatural* for her to be *saying* it. This is author-contrived. While everything in a story actually is contrived, nothing in it should *seem* contrived.

This narrator should simply have told the reader (stated it within her speech to her husband) that they always ate at seven, as: "You could have phoned," I told him irritably. We always ate at seven. Bob knew I'd have everything waiting. "If you'd think of me once in a while," I went on . . .

If you are careful and honest when you read through your story, you can't help but stumble on such mistakes. And, as you practice and work over your speeches, you can't help but become smoother and more natural.

And remember that just because you have two or more people engaged in a conversation doesn't mean everything has to be in quotes. Mere bits of dialogue give the impression of much talking.

Keep Your Words Simple

KEEP YOUR WORDS SIMPLE! This can't be said too often. Telling a story in simple, common, ordinary, everyday language is apparently neither natural nor easy for the average beginner. He says:

> "No one ever dreamed we were as poor as we were. My mother *fashioned* my clothes . . ."

This story was full of such pretentious, unnatural words and phrases, yet the author, himself, talks like everybody else. If he had been *telling* the story to me, instead of *writing* it for possible publication, he would have said: ". . . my mother *made* my clothes . . ."

Strive to tell your story as naturally as possible. Then, when it is finished and after you have checked through it for all the other points, go through it again to test your words. Wherever a simpler, shorter, more common word can be used to replace a long, unusual word, fix it. An unusual word is unusual even though most people *know* it, *if* it is a word the average person doesn't frequently use in his *conversation*. If you mean *cruel*, don't say *diabolic*. Don't say, "he labored" or "he toiled"; say, "he *worked*." And so on . . . *Choose the simplest, most common word!* And watch your narrator's thoughts. Don't let her express the theme in high-flown, flowery language. Boil it down to everyday expressions and parallels.

Never forget that your narrator is telling the story!

PREVIEWING

This is a convenient trick to help the writer condense.

A PREVIEW SENTENCE (or PARAGRAPH, depending on the individual need) frankly *tells* the reader what happened next in the chronology. This is sometimes called *foreshadowing*. Besides its main purpose (tightening the writing), it creates a feeling of *suspense* and *unity*.

What it adds up to is a great *transition!*

After you've *told* — frankly, flatly stated what happened — you *show* it in a dramatized scene, complete with dialogue, pictures, action, and emotion.

This technique is used more frequently in the character-type story, which necessarily contains more *motivating* (ELEMENT II) incidents and is, therefore, harder to keep within the short story wordage. The *previewing* method makes it possible to eliminate many otherwise necessary, but boring words that could make the difference between a sale and a rejection.

I will point out examples of this technique in the two reprinted stories, particularly in the character story.

CHAPTER VIII

EXCEPTIONS AND VARIATIONS

The exceptions are those stories that deal with off-trail subject matter, propounding and upholding such unpopular points of view as bigotry or atheism or some phase of abnormal sex, to name a few; or those that do not contain all of the ten elements.

Among this last group are those stories with unhappy endings, eliminating Element X. This type is not a good bet for a beginner as everyone prefers a happy ending — and especially a reader who has come to know and understand and sympathize with the narrator. Then there are other stories wherein the narrator has no chance to make a decision or plan. She is thrust into a situation that offers her no choice whatever. This eliminates Element IV. My objection here is that any story is stronger if the narrator dominates *by her own will* the ensuing action which leads into the climax. Others eliminate Element VI. In such a story the narrator has a plan but never gets a chance to put it into action because the climax comes about too quickly.

And there are rare instances of stories without Character Flaw. Such a story occasionally gets by because the problem or situation is of such timely, universal interest with such an unusually inspiring solution that the message for the reader exists without a character reformation on the part of the narrator. But such a story has a very limited market in the confession field. The confession editors strongly favor the tradition that the "I" in the story be guilty of some sin or transgression — and that that "I" be responsible for the trouble.

I call these types of stories exceptions because one finds them only occasionally and because they don't adhere, as do the majority of confession stories, to any specific set of rules.

A *variation* of my pattern that is occasionally used is the story that embodies the ten elements but is narrated by the *victim* of the one who possesses the Character Flaw and whose Misguided Actions bring about the Tragic Results. The narrator has the Problem, which is caused by her close relationship to the Wrong-Doer. A Theme is realized by the narrator, who either has no lesson to learn or who learns it vicariously. The Wrong-Doer generally neither reforms nor finds Happiness, but is left completely out in the cold at the story's end. As I say, the ten elements are contained in the story, but they are *divided between the two chief characters.* As I see it, the reason for this variation is either that the Wrong-Doer is so hopelessly bad there would be too little occasion for reader sympathy and identification if he were the narrator — or that the Wrong-Doer does not come to a happy end and, thus, a certain amount of reader satisfaction is lost. So the victim becomes the narrator, and the reader sympathizes with his subjugation, rejoices with his ultimate freedom, and is satisfied with the Theme that showed why the Wrong-Doer finally lost out.

The beginner who attempts this type of story must be careful that his characters are not the stock villains or long-suffering heroines of fiction that are completely outdated. All confession editors are eager and anxious for intensely human characters, which I have found to be more readily achieved by adapting the narrator and her problem, etc., to the elements in the usual way.

I only mention these types here so that the beginner can recognize them when he reads them and will not be confused because they are "different." Beyond this, however, I feel that the wise beginner will not concern himself with the exceptions and occasionally used variations. He will concentrate on mastering the most standard story, which, in the confession field, is the one that consists of the ten elements and a narrator who exemplifies them first-hand, and thereby increase his chances of a sale. The old cliche about having to learn the rules before being able to break them successfully is a safe policy to follow.

As I mentioned earlier in the chapter on PLOTTING, all of the elements cannot be equally stressed in each story. But don't confuse *emphasis* with *wordage*. A story can easily emphasize Problem (Element III) but devote most of its wordage to Motivation (Element II). Some problem-type stories will require much wordage for Element VI, while others will require only a paragraph for this element. The amount of proportional wordage needed for each element can be determined only by the material in your particular plot. For instance, if a great deal of planting is necessary to put over your actions and reactions and occurrences in a convincing and realistic manner, then Element II will have to be long and fully developed. You will find this to be the case with a great many *problem-type* confession stories.

But the long, fully developed motivation (or background story) does not necessarily mean that the immediate problem isn't the focal point (sometimes called the *Central Drive*) of the story.

The most frequently published stories emphasize either PROBLEM or CHARACTER FLAW. This difference in emphasis changes a story so completely one would, at first glance, find it hard to believe that the two types follow the same, one pattern.

Because the *problem-emphasized* story is the most popular and because it is the easiest for the average beginner to master, I have used this type consistently in my examples throughout this book. And because the suggested presentation (opening with ELEMENT III, flashing back to ELEMENT II, then forward again and on with ELEMENT IV and straight through to the end in the order in which the elements are listed) is the easiest way to put over a story, I have, so far, developed the sample plots in this manner.

I say "easiest" because a problem-opening immediately catches the reader's interest. And by fully developing and dramatizing this opening situation, the author is able to leave the reader with a feeling of suspense and anticipation when he takes him back through the less dramatic and less urgent background of the narrator's life. Flashback enables the author to speed up and skip through the very necessary but less intriguing background data.

However, this manner of presenting the *problem-emphasized* story is not by any means a hard and fast rule, and sometimes the story itself will suggest, or even demand, another starting place. There are stories that begin way back with the narrator's first six-year-old recollections of her days in the orphanage when she first began to get the way she is when her final problem presents itself. The trouble with this is it's too easy to tell your story in 20,000 boring words instead of 6,000 salable words. You have no easy shortcuts. There are others that begin after the whole story is all over and solved. But when you begin at the very end, it's harder to snag your reader's interest. After all, it *is* all over, and there isn't any immediate suspense.

Sometimes a slight rearrangement of elements is necessary. Perhaps in your story, the narrator's decision will have to be made instantly. Then ELEMENT II would *have* to follow ELEMENT IV. Or maybe, because of the nature of your climax, your narrator will have to realize the theme before she can make restitution. The order of the appearance of the elements in the writing of the story is flexible. The presentation of them I suggested in my samples, however, is the most usual and the most natural for the *problem-emphasized* story.

The *character-emphasized* story is different only in that it emphasizes the Character Flaw instead of the Problem. In a *problem-emphasized* story, the problem was not necessarily caused by the narrator's basic Character Flaw. Examples of this would be the sudden need for the narrator's mother-in-law to live with them — or her husband's adolescent child by his former marriage; or the sudden threat of an old-buried secret coming out; or the unbearable death of a child to be endured. . . These things would have happened if the narrator hadn't had any flaw at all. Of course, because she does have a flaw — which she must have because this is a confession story — she MISHANDLES her problem (ELEMENT IV).

In a *character-emphasized* story, there wouldn't have been any problem at all if it hadn't been for the narrator's flaw. Because in this type of story it is the flaw that creates the problem.

That's why this type of story can often be told chronologically, beginning with an incident that shows the narrator's flaw in action.

There may be an opening paragraph or two of introduction by the narrator, in which she sums up the whole trouble in some such manner as this: *Grandpa always used to say to mother, "Nora's greed will ruin her life if you don't curb it." But mother didn't curb it, and I didn't see how my life could be ruined when I knew how to get what I wanted . . .* This sort of opening is a kind of crutch. The author has told the reader the crux of the whole trouble and hinted at tragedy ahead of the narrator because of her greed. And thus, a certain amount of reader-suspense has been aroused. After this brief, "introductory" opening, the narrator swings into Element II, which can serve either one of two purposes. It can show the reasons for the narrator's developing this Character Flaw, or if the flaw is one that is so prevalent among people it needs no *special* (everything needs *some*) *reason* to make it understandable and acceptable to the reader, Element II shows the contributing factors (or lack of correction) as the flaw develops.

Or the author might open this type of story (*Character-emphasized*) with Element IX — where everything seems completely hopeless. The narrator knows at last why and where she was wrong, she has realized the theme, and she has learned her lesson, but, it seems, too late! She has lost the one thing she wanted most. Then, after establishing this hopeless situation, the author swings back, and the story proceeds chronologically, beginning with Element II, whether it be to motivate the flaw or to show its development, and so on through to the end of the story where Element X comes about in one form or another to change her situation or attitude from what it was in the opening scene.

I prefer this latter presentation for this type of story because your suspense is ready-made, and, since your theme is already brought out, unity is almost automatically achieved. The story is told in a series of incidents, each of which is dominated by the narrator's Character Flaw.

All of the elements are here, but the immediate problem (ELEMENT III) is not emphasized; it is presented, rather, as the final incident that leads into such disastrous consequences the narrator is forced to see the theme. Often this type of story runs to novelette or magazine book length.

These two types of stories appear to be so different, *because of the shift in emphasis,* it is hard to believe, until you take them apart, that they are both made up of the same ten elements.

After you have learned to write one type, you can just as easily write the other. Your personal preference, your particular plot, and the magazine to which you want to slant your story will determine which element you emphasize and the manner in which you present your story.

So the next step, after reading this book, is to read several issues of all the confession magazines. After you have selected those that appeal to you personally more than others, study all the stories in them and practice breaking them down into the elements. All of the magazines publish both types, but you will find that some lean more toward one, while others seem to prefer the other type.

If you give them all a thorough reading, however, before you make your selections, you can't go wrong. Because you will choose those that prefer the type of story you prefer reading and are, therefore, most *naturally* inclined to write.

CHAPTER IX

THE STORY BEHIND MY PROBLEM STORY

I chose this story — "My Selfish Man" — to use as an example of the PROBLEM story in this book because it is so typical in a *timeless* way. In other words, it doesn't have any of the currently popular ingredients (sex, youth, and violence) nor is it sensational or tear-jerking, nor is there anything especially new about it — in the current-happening-now sense. But it is the kind of story that always was salable and undoubtedly always will be . . . Because it's a marriage story with a universal lesson for practically every woman of every age who is married!

The idea for it came to me one afternoon, when I dropped in on an old friend and found her in such a despondent mood that the bad, sad news spilled right out of her . . . News about her pretty eighteen-year-old daughter's decision to set up housekeeping with her twenty-one-year-old boyfriend *without marriage*. "Because they're in love," my friend told me, "and because he's convinced her that when you're married, you feel trapped — and that kills love." Her lips twisted scornfully. "And when you don't have that *legal strangle-hold,* as they call it, you have to keep pleasing each other."

Her voice kept wobbling. "I couldn't stop her, and she's gone."

"A lot of kids are doing that nowadays," I said comfortingly, but I couldn't keep from shuddering. And I could see she wasn't comforted. "She'll come to her senses," I added inanely. "After the example you and Matt have set —"

"That's just it," she interrupted. "She said she didn't want the kind of dull, loveless, routine *legal arrangement* her father and I have." She held up her palms, her eyes full of tears and bewilderment. "But isn't that bound to happen after all the years and children and struggles?" I nodded. It *had* happened in every *older* marriage I could think of! "I tried to make her see why we women have to have the security of those legal marriage certificates," she added.

I knew then I had a plot, and as soon as I got home I started working with it. I spent a lot of time and paper trying to make that girl, whom I'll call *Judy*, my narrator. But I couldn't make it click that way. If I used the "common law" marriage as the Wrong Decision (ELEMENT IV), then I had a too routine trial marriage story, which would have to end in failure and disillusionment . . . Because the confession market does not (currently) sanction this non-legal kind of "marriage."

I kept thinking about it, twisting the situation this way and that way, and I remembered again my friend's defensive words — that the years and the children and the struggles were bound to take some of the love out of a marriage. "I tried to make her see why we women have to have the security of those legal marriage certificates." Because in too many cases it was the only thing that kept their husbands with them, was what she meant. But surely that wasn't fair

or right. And it was then that I suddenly knew *this* woman
— my friend, Judy's mother — was going to be my narrator
... Because she was the "typical" married woman who was
expecting and tolerating a deteriorating marriage relationship — who was using her marriage certificate as a kind of
manacle. And by the same token, the woman without that
security, Judy, would have to keep pleasing her man — to
keep him with her. Because *he* wasn't trapped!

So it was suddenly obvious that Judy and her lover, whom
I'll call Paul, would be the Climax (ELEMENT VII) to show
this "typical" married woman that she is abusing her marriage contract. I'll call my narrator *Laura*, and it will be her
discovery that Judy — who will not be her daughter now,
but one of her peer group — is not legally married. And if
this discovery comes as the Climax, it has to be a shocking
and unexpected revelation — which then means that it was
a secret before, with Judy and Paul pretending to be really
married.

Therefore, since Judy's *arrangement* can't be an open de-
fiance of the established custom, as it was in the real Judy's
case, why *aren't* they legally married? It's obvious to me now
that they should WANT to be, but CAN'T. And the obvious
reason for this would be the inability of one of them to get
a divorce. So, because Judy is living in a secret *common law*
situation, she has to keep her husband happier with her than
other women who have their husbands legally trapped.

Other *women*, I was thinking. Not *just* Laura! Because it
isn't *only* Laura's story, since Laura represents the average
woman. Judy, on the other hand, is the exception! So now I
knew I needed a couple of other typical wives who are con-
centrating on their own happiness instead of that of their

husbands . . . Because they feel safe and secure with their marriages! Because their husbands are stuck with them in a way Paul isn't stuck with Judy! I decided to make Laura (and her friends) as young as I could and still enable her to have the necessary years of marriage and children and a lot of struggles behind her.

I knew I had it then, and I knew the time had come to fit it into the ten elements — so I could see where the remaining holes were . . .

I. She has the mistaken attitude that because the husband is stuck with the marriage contract, the wife can let down, i.e., as opposed to the courtship period, now she can be what she wants to be, not what he wants her to be — because she's got him hooked with the legal marriage license.

II. The popularly accepted fact that love does get dull and routine after the years and children and struggles — IF YOU DON'T CONSCIOUSLY COUNTERACT IT; in here go all the facts that lead up to the opening — in this case, I will need the specific details in the stories of each of the other women who play a vital role in the narrator's story, i.e., the two *like* Laura, and Judy, the good example!

III. Her chronic blue mood lately because she and her husband are not happy together anymore, not pulling in the same direction. (I don't have the mechanical device that is going to give this problem immediacy.)

IV. I don't have this yet either — because it relates to the Device.

V. I don't know this yet either — because it depends on IV.

VI.   This will be all the action that will result from her
        Wrong Decision — AND everything else that will be
        necessary to lead to

VII. The shocking discovery that Judy and Paul aren't
        married. This causes her to realize that Paul stays
        because he WANTS to, and this, in turn, leads her to
        the uncomfortable question: would HER husband
        stay with her IF HE HAD A CHOICE?

VIII. Now, understanding why Judy put Paul's happiness
        ahead of her own, she can also understand how the
        three of them (she and the other two wives like her,
        whom I'll name *Pat* and *Claire*) have disappointed
        their husbands, have stopped being the women they
        were when their husbands *wanted* to marry them. No
        wonder their husbands don't like them very much
        anymore — they'd thought they were getting some-
        body completely different! She sees that the only
        way to keep the love in your marriage is to keep
        putting *his* happiness first, the way you did when
        you were trying to get him to propose — *the way
        Judy has to!*

IX.   Now she's going to start pleasing her husband in
        every way she can, putting his happiness ahead of
        hers, the way she did when they were going together
        and he was so in love with her.

X.   This happy ending will show that her new resolution
        was very successful.

*   *   *

Now I can see clearly what I do have and what I don't
have. And these are the details I still have to work out:

1. A mechanical device that brings her problem to a head and necessitates an immediate decision.
2. A wrong decision that will lead directly to the climax, i.e., to her accidental discovery of Judy's lack of a marriage certificate.
3. HOW is she going to make this discovery?
4. I need specific ways to create an active conflict between Laura and her husband APART FROM the years and the children and the struggles.
5. I need a *different* situation with each of the other two wives who are also going to illustrate this FLAW. (I don't, however, have to resolve *their* problems; I just have to make sure the narrator understands their failures as well as hers by the time the story ends.)
6. I need a gimmick to get these particular four women together — so that I will have a logical reason to explain them in detail to the reader and keep them together.
7. In my specific details I need to show HOW these three factors — the years and the children and the struggles — really do contribute to the deterioration of a marriage.
8. Since the narrator learns her lesson as the result of the Climax, everything after this (her reformation and the tying up of all loose ends) is anti-climactic and must be written as briefly as possible.

However, since in *this* story it would *logically* take both time and incidents for her to *undo* the damage to her marriage from years of neglect, I will show my Happy Ending in an EPILOGUE. This is a very popular device to accomplish this purpose.

Remembering what I said about each short story being

strong on a couple of the elements and weak on the rest (with all represented, however), you will notice that *this* story is strong on II, VII, and VIII.

Before I begin to write I'm going to work out every single detail pertaining to my characters and to my plot. In the finished story, reprinted in the next chapter, I'll indicate the ELEMENTS and these POINTS to show you how it all did work out, along with a few other examples of the writing techniques I've discussed in earlier chapters.

And, incidentally, I would like to point out here that a whole new, different story could emerge from this idea by simply changing the narrator. To Steve perhaps. Or Judy. Or Paul. Or even an older Lynn, who could, as the baby-sitter, inadvertently discover this shocking secret. Can you see that by making the same basic situation another character's story you would automatically end up with a totally new plot?

Chapter X

"MY SELFISH MAN"

From: Revealing Romances
(January 1969)

1. That Friday got off to its usual tense start, with the four of us at the breakfast table, all of us stewing silently with our own problems.

2. Steve was sipping his coffee behind the sports page, still sulking because the camper he'd wanted to buy that had been such a big bargain had been sold yesterday — to somebody else.

3. My own thoughts were wandering ahead to the brunch I was having for Pat and Claire and Judy. Pat was on another one of her civic kicks — this time she had a petition to be signed — and I'd foolishly offered to get us all together here to organize it. I wished it were behind me instead of ahead.

1: *Element* I

2: *Point* 4

3 *and* 4:
Point 6.

I was sick of Pat's problems, and Claire depressed me lately, and I never had really felt comfortable with Judy.

4. Lynn — pretty and fourteen and boy crazy was pouting because Steve had said a loud, final no to her weekend invitation to Crystal Lake that included her current crush. And it was because he was too selfish to postpone our dull two-week vacation for even three days to make it possible.

4 *thru* 6:
Point 4.

5. I shuddered at the dreary prospect of those two weeks. Every single year for the past fifteen years we dutifully divided two weeks between our parents' farms. It meant so much to Steve he always had to get started the day after the kids' school was out. Just once I'd have liked a week at some glamorous resort-hotel where I could get dressed up and dance and bask in a lot of luxury. But even though you could take the boy out of the country, I thought for the thousandth time, you couldn't take the country out of the boy. It was sure different with girls, though — with me, anyway. As far back as I could remember, I'd waited for the day I could get to the city, and now, every year after those two annual weeks, I was always relieved to be back.

6. "Mom." It was a plaintive cry from twelve-year-old Terry. He gave me a pleading glance. "Don't forget —"

6 and 7:
Element III
(device) and
Point 1.

7. I cut him off with a reassuring smile and took a deep breath. "Steve," I said softly. He glared at me from around the paper, and I pushed on. "Today's the deadline for Terry's camp application, hon." The deadline for his father's signature and check. Steve had stalled along on it because he'd wanted the camper for family weekends — miserable, uncomfortable, camping weekends I'd fought tooth and nail against. Now, though, the camper threat was over. And Terry's two weeks in August up in the North Woods wasn't interfering with Steve's two precious weeks. "His whole troop's going, Steve," I added.

8. He gave in with an unpleasant grunt, and Terry's whole face lit up. "It's on the mantel," he said eagerly, pushing his chair back.

9. "Sit still," Steve growled, "and finish your breakfast." He rattled his paper, hiding behind it again.

10. I gave Terry a warning glance. This wasn't the time to push Steve. I'd catch him after he finished breakfast. "I'll bring it to school this afternoon, honey," I whispered to Terry.

10: Plant for
Element VII

11. Then Lynn had to add fuel to the smoldering tension with a muttered, "Everybody's getting what they want out of this summer except me."

12. I shushed her and was relieved Steve either didn't hear or chose to ignore her. A few minutes later the kids left for school without another ruckus — Terry hopefully; Lynn with a glum expression. I'd let her have a big barbecue for her gang when we got back, I thought. Then I wondered resentfully why I always had to be the umpire in the family, keeping the surface peace, finding ways to soften the kids' disappointments or, when I could, finding devious ways to get around Steve to get them what they wanted — or what *I* wanted.

12: Element III.

13. Steve was sticking another piece of bread in the toaster when the phone rang. I hurried into the hall to get it. It was Pat from next door, sounding bright and efficient, asking if I'd gotten hold of the others. I told her I had. "They're coming at eleven," I said.

13 thru 15:
Point 6.

14. "I'll come a little early," she said in a smug, mysterious voice. "I got the detective's report, Laura."

15. I said that was fine, not asking about it. It was obviously good news. We hung up, and when I got back to the

kitchen, Steve was standing, ready to leave, his face tightened into a scowl.

16. "You're too lax with Lynn," he shot at me. "The kid's got nothing on her mind but boys."

16 *thru* 19: *Point* 4.

17. I stiffened, resenting his taking out his own disappointment on the rest of us. "What should she have on it?" I demanded snappishly. "Cows and pigs and chickens?"

18. "A summer with her grandparents might straighten her out," he said coldly as he edged past me toward the hall. "Think it over, Laura."

19. He left, and I shouted after him, "I think I understand a fourteen-year-old girl better than you do!"

20. The door slammed, and I looked around bewilderedly at my pretty coppertone kitchen, at the nicely furnished living room beyond. How hard we'd worked for our spacious, modern house in one of Chicago's nicest suburbs. Why, I wondered suddenly, did marriages have to deteriorate into ugly scenes when you stopped struggling for things? But, of course, it was the years together, not the struggles, that did it. Next fall it would be sixteen years for us. In the beginning you think it's going to be so different.

20 *and* 21: *Lead-in to Flashback.*

21. I thought about getting the bowl of fresh fruit and the strudel ready and taking out the big electric percolater and getting dressed. But I didn't. I sank back down in the chair and poured myself another cup of coffee and let my thoughts drift back to the Steve I'd been so madly in love with so long ago.

22. We'd met in the big downtown insurance company where we both worked. Steve was two months fresh out of college, and I was two months fresh out of high school, both of us fresh off our farms. Steve had left his folks' wheat farm in Iowa reluctantly because his two older, married brothers were already settled on it, and there wasn't enough in it for all of them. I'd left my parents' dairy farm in Wisconsin because I hated every single thing about farm life. But our different reasons for being in the city didn't seem important then. All that mattered was our sharing similar backgrounds, because it made the bond that took us past the first quick physical attraction.

22 thru 72: Element II.

Point 4.

23. We had a magic summer of discovery — of each other and the big, exciting city. I revelled in every sooty, crowded little speck of it. Steve conceded that it might be all right to live in one of

the suburbs — "As long as you were
there with me," he said softly.

24. We each got a week off that fall, and
we were married in the City Hall. We
spent three days of our honeymoon
week with my folks and three days
with Steve's. When we got back to our
little furnished apartment, Steve said
wistfully, "We can go back for two
weeks every summer."

25. I was so glad to be back in the city
that I agreed happily. Two weeks out
of fifty-two seemed such a small piece
of time.

26. The years rolled back around me —
the happy years and the unhappy ones.
And now what? Were these the indifferent years? The stale, separate years?
They weren't actively unhappy, but
they weren't really happy, either, I
was suddenly realizing.

27. That first year, when I kept my job
and we scrimped and dreamed and
laughed and made ecstatic love — that
must have been our golden year. That
next year, when Lynn came to us, was
filled with tenderness and wonder. Two
more years brought Terry and a better,
bigger apartment. They were busy,
happy years, still full of love and sharing and growing together. The next

two years were the unhappy ones, with my miscarriage and six months after that the news of my older sister's death. It was a sad summer at the farm that year. But Steve and I were still together in every way.

28. We were married seven years before we could afford our own house, but we were glad we'd waited for what we wanted. Those were the settling, fulfilling years. Steve wasn't around as much any more. He was working hard and getting involved in local civic affairs. It was all building toward the time when he'd be able to open his own brokerage. But I was busy, too, with my separate affairs — the P.T.A. and my big house and my new friends.

29. Pat Selby, who lived right next door, was my favorite friend. We'd hit it off right from the start, though there was a lot of pity mixed in with my affection. That first year it was pity because after five years of marriage she was still yearning for her first child. That next spring when she did finally get pregnant, I was almost as happy as she was. It was all we talked about all summer — the nursery, the layette, the books and rules, names, and all the dreams ahead. If I sometimes thought Wayne, her

29 thru 42: Point 5.

handsome husband, seemed a little bored with it all, I told myself it would all change when the baby was here.

30. "Maybe," Pat said once, "he'll be so crazy about his son he'll even want a desk job in the city." She sounded so wistful I wished he would, too. But I didn't share her hope. Wayne liked traveling all week for a wholesale hardware concern, and when he got home weekends, he wanted to live it up. He just wasn't the homebody type.

31. Nothing worked out for Pat. That winter, two weeks before the baby was due, a serious kidney complication developed, and she was rushed to the hospital. The awful result was an operation that made future babies impossible. The final shattering grief was the loss of her little son two days later. It was a sad time for all of us, it was devastating for Pat. But more than anybody — Wayne included — Claire and I seemed able to comfort her. Maybe it was because out of our whole neighborhood crowd, we two could really understand, with me having lost a baby and Claire not able to have any of her own, either.

32. Claire Anderson lived two blocks away. Our friendship had started when one of her little stepdaughters, Vivian, and my Lynn, both in second grade, be-

came such bosom pals. I wasn't as fond
of Claire as I was Pat, though. A former
schoolteacher, she'd married late, and
she'd married a widower with two little
girls. It was her aggressiveness, her
bossiness that sometimes annoyed me.
And she was vain and conceited — at
least I'd thought that in the beginning.
But Steve liked big Gus Anderson. They
played golf together at our local free
course and went to the prize fights and
ball games and argued about politics.
So with our little girls always together,
too, Claire and I were thrown together
a lot, and as I understood her better, I
liked her more.

33. I slowly began to realize how much
Gus still lived in the memories of his
dead wife — and how much it hurt
Claire. And I saw how he used Claire
to mother his daughters and make a
home for them all — but not to really
be a mother. I saw that the second time
Steve and I were over there for bridge.
Their children had been put to bed,
but little Erica, only four then, had
sneaked downstairs and demanded
something to eat.

34. Claire's voice was gentle but firm. "I'll
warm up those carrots you didn't eat,
honey," she said.

35. The child's eyes filled with tears, and

she ran to Gus, crying, "No! I want ice cream."

36. Claire insisted quietly, "No ice cream until you eat your vegetables." She reached for Erica, but Gus held her, glaring at Claire.

37. Steve and I were both shocked at the coldness in his eyes and voice when he said, "Margaret didn't believe in forcing her children to eat anything." He stood up, carrying the child. "Nor in starving them," he added cruelly. Steve and I waited in stunned silence while he took the child into the kitchen and gave her the ice cream.

38. Claire shrugged. "And then he expects me to keep them well," she said in a brittle, indifferent voice to no one in particular. But I saw the hurt and fear in her eyes, and I understood her better after that.

39. I saw a lot of her hurts after that, but that was the one I remembered a year later, the day she said to Pat, "Every woman wants a child, Pat, but you don't have to *have* it. I couldn't love Gus's little girls more if they were mine." The heartache was in the way she still thought of them as Gus's children.

40. It was right after that that Pat began talking about adopting and trying to sell

Wayne on the idea, then crying in my kitchen because Wayne wouldn't hear of it. "He says he was willing to have his own, but not somebody else's," she moaned. "He says we can have a real great life without any." She made a wry face. "If I travel with him."

41. I never knew what to say. I couldn't tell her I thought Wayne was selfish and unfair. And I certainly couldn't tell her how much I pitied her.

42. Another year went by, and Pat did stop brooding. She got very busy serving on all sorts of civic committees on behalf of children and working on a volunteer basis for a nearby orphanage, often bringing a different youngster home with her for an overnight visit. She hadn't stopped trying to persuade Wayne to adopt a child; she'd just changed her tactics.

43. Those next two years were rough for us, with Steve going into business for himself. That first year the all-consuming problem of scrimping and budgeting and making ends meet was aggravated by having Steve operating from home, tying up the phone, demanding quiet, keeping all of us on tenterhooks with his irregular hours. The second year we were still scrimp-

43: *Plant for Element* VII *and Point* 3.

ing, but Steve had gotten enough business to support his own office in our local shopping center. Actually, he and another independent broker shared the setup, each with his own private cubicle but sharing the reception room and the girl Friday.

44. Paul Harper was one of Steve's first big customers. The Harpers had recently moved across the street at the end of our block, and that summer they moved in, Steve and Paul had found a mutual interest in Paul's small truck garden. It was the frustrated farmer in Steve. I'd seen Judy around, and we'd exchanged a few words at the supermarket, but we had nothing in common beyond that.

44 thru 56:
Point 5 and
Plant for VII.

45. After Steve wrote a big, expensive life insurance policy for Paul, he wanted me to have them over to dinner, and after that we were invited over there. It got so every time I had the girls over, Steve would say, "Is Judy coming, too?" He'd say it in almost an accusing manner, as if I might be shirking my duty or something.

46. His wanting to force Judy into everything made me mad. He insisted that Lynn babysit for their children — Jill, a toddler then, and Gregory, a small

baby — every time the four of us went anywhere. And he wanted Judy always included.

47. Once I told him, "She doesn't have anything in common with the rest of us."

48. But that made him mad, and he retorted, "Not catty enough for the rest of you?"

49. I was hurt and puzzled by his defense of her and attack on me. It wasn't that I didn't like her, though. It was just that I felt uncomfortable with her — we all did. She was too sweet — and too submissive to Paul. Her frank, open adoration of him was somehow embarrassing, and in a funny way it was kind of insulting, too. It was as if she were married to somebody so much more special than anybody else. Every time we were over there, she waited on him hand and foot. She wore her straight ash-blond hair unbecomingly hanging to her shoulders — because Paul liked it that way. She wore dowdy-looking housedresses instead of slacks, the way the rest of us did, because Paul didn't like women in pants. She deferred to his every wish when it came to their children, and in every other way, too. Paul was her god. It was Paul says this

and Paul says that until the rest of us wanted to scream.

50. "The guy acts like God," Claire said once after we'd dropped Judy off. "He takes it all as his due."

51. The three of us had been shopping in one of the big department stores for a joint baby shower gift for one of the girls in our neighborhood. On our way out we'd stopped to look at a big wig display. Claire had impulsively plunked a gorgeous pale blond one on Judy's head, and we'd all exclaimed admiringly over the effect. Judy's eyes were round with delight as she gazed in the mirror at her stunning reflection, and I'd said, "You really should have your hair lightened."

52. Her eyes clouded as she took it off. "Paul wouldn't like it," she said wistfully. "He doesn't like anything artificial."

53. Claire gave me a disgusted look. "Don't you ever want to do or be anything just because *you* want to?" she asked Judy, her voice sharply critical.

54. But Judy's smile was sweet, and her answer was typical. "The only thing I really want is to keep Paul happy."

55. It was the way she put his needs and wants ahead of the kids even that an-

noyed Pat. "If those babies were mine,"
Pat said once, "I'd make a playground
out of that dumb vegetable garden of
his." Pat said that on our way home
from Judy's the day she slapped Jill
just for pulling up one of Paul's carrots.
"No woman should spoil a man like
that."

56. But Judy never complained about
Paul — or about anything. And for all
the surface intimacy among us, we
didn't really know anything about them.
We knew they'd come from someplace
in California and that neither of them
had any close family. And they were
both disgustingly thrifty. Take the vegetable garden, for example. And the
cheap, simple clothes Judy made for
herself and the kids. They didn't have
any decent furniture, just bargain odds
and ends, with Paul making a lot of it
himself. And he drove an old jalopy that
wasn't even running half the time. And
when Judy marketed, she ran all over to
save a few pennies.

57. It wasn't that I blamed anybody for
being broke. Steve and I had certainly
been strapped when he was getting
started on his own. But Paul and Judy
didn't have to live like that. As an elec-
trician for a big building contractor,

57: *Plant for
Element* VII.

we knew Paul made good, steady wages. And there *was* that big life policy. It just didn't make sense. But they were both so reserved that it kept us from asking any personal questions — which was all right. Only, how could we feel like close friends?

58. The years seemed to disappear fast. Steve's business took hold and thrived, and we got a second car. And we kept making our annual visits to the farms. Our folks and kids got older, and our marriage got duller, though you don't see that happening. You just suddenly one day discover that somewhere along the way you lost something — the spark between you, I guess, that got it all started in the first place.

    58: *Point 7.*

59. I'll never forget the shattering way it happened to Pat last March, seven years after she lost her baby. It seemed as if nothing had changed at all. She was still trying to interest Wayne in a child and in a desk job. But they were still childless, and Wayne was still traveling. That weekend she'd "borrowed" a little six-year-old orphan named Sammy who had big brown eyes just like Wayne's.

    59: *Transition.* *Preview (tell). Plant (for Pat's discovery).*

60. Wayne had been nice to him, showing more interest than usual, but he'd stub-

    60 *thru* 62: *Preview (show).*

bornly refused to consider taking him into their home for more than the week-end, even on a trial basis. So they drove him back to the Home, and much later that night, after Wayne was asleep, Pat sneaked downstairs and opened his sample case to slip in a snapshot of Sammy where Wayne would be sure to find it. She had some crazy idea that, alone and lonely in an impersonal hotel room, the reminder of the little boy who looked so much like him might change his mind.

61. But Pat was in for the shock of her life when she found the tiny gift-wrapped box with the card addressed to Rosemary. Inside, Wayne had written, "Happy Birthday, darling." She'd unwrapped it carefully and found a pair of exquisite pearl earrings. Horrified and furious and scared, she'd still had sense enough to rewrap it and keep her secret that next morning when Wayne left.

62. "Until I have a chance to decide what to do," she told us tearfully later that morning. Claire had stopped in on her way home from driving the kids to school, so when Pat came in with her awful problem, I made a fresh pot of coffee, and the three of us hashed it over.

63. "The wife's always got the advantage in this kind of thing," I told her.

    63: Element I.

64. "Just play dumb, and she'll get tired of being the other woman," Claire suggested.

65. "But how can I go on pretending I think he still loves *me*?" Pat cried.

66. "Love," Claire scoffed harshly. "After twelve years of marriage men don't love their wives — they're just stuck."

    66: Element I.

67. It depressed me to realize Claire wasn't completely wrong. But at least Steve wasn't interested in another woman, I thought, and for once I was thankful he was so wrapped up in his business.

    67: Element I.

68. That was two months ago. A week ago Pat told me she'd hired a detective. "Because I've got to know what I'm fighting," she said miserably. It was still going on. Now that she knew, the signs were obvious.

    68: Transition. Point 4. Plant.

69. I didn't see what good it would do her to know the sordid facts, but I didn't argue with her. I was in the throes of my own battle with Steve over the camper one of his clients wanted to sell him. He wanted it so we could spend every single weekend up in the woods, where Steve and the kids could fish and hike and wallow in nature, where I could cook our meals in a dinky make-

    69: Point 4.

shift kitchen and wash our clothes by hand and be bored to death.

70. Naturally Lynn was as repelled by the whole idea as I was, and I saw to it Terry was more interested in his own plans here at home with the promise of his two weeks at camp with his own gang in August. But the more the three of us argued against it, the more stubbornly Steve wanted it, and the hotter the quarrel got, with both of us hurling accusations at each other. I listened as Steve complained about how hard he worked — and for what? And then I lost no time in reminding him of all the sacrifices I'd made — struggling for two years because he wanted to give up the security of a good, steady salary for the freedom of his own agency, being a good sport about spending every single vacation of my whole life on two miserable farms I hated. I even dredged up our friendship with Judy and Paul, whom I didn't even like, just because *he* liked them. So why couldn't *he* consider *my* feelings once in a while? He'd accuse me of spoiling the kids and turning them against the kind of values he considered worthwhile, and it kept ending up in a furious impasse.

70 *thru* 71:
Points 1, 2, 4, *and* 7.
Element IV.

71. Last night he told me the fellow had sold the darned camper. "So you don't have to worry about leaving your precious city," he said unpleasantly.

71: Lead-out of Flashback. Transition.

72. I didn't snap back. He'd sulk for a while, I knew, but by the time we made our pilgrimage to the farms, he'd have forgotten all about it, and we'd all be back to normal again. But suddenly I was wondering what was so great about our normal.

72: Element V. Ends Element II.

73. I was still at the kitchen table, struggling against my blue, discouraged feeling, when the phone shrilled again. I glanced at the kitchen clock, startled that it was nearly ten, and hurried guiltily into the hall.

74. It was Judy, telling me she was going to be a little late because she was painting her kitchen and wanted to finish the first coat. "I'll come, though," she said, "because I don't want to let Pat down, but I'm going to have to leave early. I want it all finished by the time Paul gets home, and —"

74 thru 76: Plant to motivate Element VII.

75. "But I thought Paul was going to do it tomorrow," I cut in. I'd heard him telling Steve the other night that he couldn't join the fellows for golf Saturday because he was going to paint the kitchen.

76. "It's a surprise," Judy explained. "So he can play golf tomorrow."

77. I swallowed back the quick protest that rose up in my throat, and we hung up. Then I dashed upstairs to get the beds made and the bathroom tidied, sorrier than ever I'd gotten involved in Pat's latest project.

78. It had started ten days ago when a seven-year-old child had been struck and killed at the corner of Elm Street and Hoover Avenue. There'd been a couple of editorials and some requests for a stoplight, and when the city refused, Pat had decided to get the necessary signatures on the petition. She'd enlisted the three of us to each take an area and ring doorbells, and this morning she was going to tell us all about it. I slipped into a pair of slacks and a knit shirt and tore downstairs to clean up in the kitchen.

78: Point 6.

79. I was arranging the fruit bowl when Pat came in with her maps and papers and a bright smile on her face. "Her name is Rosemary Pendleton — *Mrs.* Raymond Pendleton," she added happily. It took me a second to realize she was talking about Wayne's mistress. "She and her husband," she was rushing on, "and their two little girls —

79: Transition.
79 thru 85: Point 5.

seven and nine — live in Peoria. Isn't that marvelous, Laura?"

80. I must have looked as blank as I felt. "She's *married*," Pat explained impatiently. "And she has little kids. It means Wayne can't be thinking of asking for a divorce to marry her." She waited, her smile fading. "Doesn't it, Laura?"

81. "Of course it does," I said quickly. "It's just a fling. Men are — men are like that," I rambled along vaguely.

82. But she was reassured. She set the papers down on the coffee table and dug in her purse, handing me a snapshot. "He managed to get this. She isn't even pretty," she gloated.

83. I studied it. The woman was getting out of a car; there was a startled look on her face. She was a tall, angular woman with a very short, boyish haircut, about as different from tiny, soft Pat as night from day. "Not a bit pretty," I agreed. But there was a sensuousness about her that must have added up to a lot of sex appeal. I didn't mention that, though. Nor did I say anything about its being a funny thing to be happy about the fact that your husband may not have plans to marry the woman he is having an affair with. But it made me feel more dejected than ever.

84. I got the coffee started, and then Claire came. She was wearing a new mod-print mini-dress that looked ridiculous on her — and she had a new story to tell us to show us how attractive she was to men. When she twirled foolishly, showing off her outfit, Pat and I said it was a cute dress, which it was — for a cute sixteen-year-old girl! But there just wasn't any way we could tell Claire that her too youthful clothes and exaggerated makeup made her look even older than her thirty-five years. So we just listened politely to her account of how the cleaning man had mistaken her for Vivian this morning. "He said he didn't see how my husband could tell the three of us apart."

85. I forced a smile, but I felt more like crying. If Gus weren't so cold and critical toward her, I thought pityingly, she wouldn't have such a desperate need for approval. I explained why Judy was going to be late, and while they made the usual cracks — Claire declaring that *she* wouldn't grovel the way Judy did, not for any man, and Pat saying if she were as pretty as Judy, she'd have Paul waiting on *her* — I heated up the apple strudel.   86: *Point 6.*

86. I'd just gotten everything on the table when Judy came in, scrubbed and

pretty and sweet and smudged here and there with bits of yellow paint. We ate and talked about our kids and husbands and houses, and then we drifted into the living room and got down to Pat's business. Each of us got our territory and our petition to be signed and the facts we were to recite to each housewife. We all had a lot of questions, and it took a lot of time. "We've only got a week to get this into the next council meeting," Pat said. And we all agreed to work as fast as we could.

87: *Transition.*
Plant.

87. When our gathering finally broke up, I felt relieved. Judy left first — to get her painting finished before Paul got home — and a few minutes later Pat and Claire left. My blue mood was still hanging over me while I straightened up. I was putting the papers Pat had left with me temporarily out of the way on the mantel when I saw Terry's camp application. It was still unsigned, still without Steve's check, and I'd told Terry I'd bring it to school. But Steve had left in a huff again — over Lynn this morning — and it had been overlooked.

87 *thru* 91:
Motivation for otherwise coincidental Element VII.

88. I looked distractedly at the clock, feeling unreasonably angry with Steve for stalling on it until the last minute. If I

hurried, I decided, I could get to Steve's office and still make it to school before Terry left.

89. I hurried, but the traffic was heavy, and then I had trouble finding a parking place. I rushed breathlessly into the office, and Steve wasn't even there.

90. "He just went across the street for cigarettes," Shirley, his secretary, told me. "Why don't you just go on in the office and wait for him?"

91. Her desk was piled high with forms, and she looked busy, so I didn't want to hold her up. I went on inside, sinking down into Steve's big swivel chair. There was a lot of opened mail and policies scattered messily around on his desk.

92. At first I wasn't interested or curious, and I certainly didn't mean to pry. It must have been pure reflex habit that caused me to start straightening things, because I wasn't even aware I was doing it. All my thoughts were on Terry's application in my purse and my irritation with Steve for having to be constantly nagged for every little thing.

93. That was how the return name and address on one of the envelopes happened to catch my eye — Paul Harper, 708 Maple Street. The policy and the pre-

93 *thru* 101: *Element* VII.

mium notice and the check were all clipped to the empty envelope. I still wouldn't have thought anything about it, though, if I hadn't noticed the amount of the check. It seemed such an unusually big amount for people like Judy and Paul. No wonder Steve had been so thrilled seven years ago when Paul had taken it out! So I did deliberately look at the policy then. As I read on, my bewilderment turned to stunned horror.

94. The policy was made out to Paul Brooke Hamilton, also known as Paul Harper. I could hardly breathe as I read on. Beneficiary: Miss Judith Anne Gregory, common-law wife of Paul Brooke Hamilton. Underneath her name were the words, "Also known as Mrs. Paul Harper." As the meaning gradually penetrated my shocked brain, my horror spread. Harper wasn't really their name; they weren't really married. Judy's last name was really Gregory — Gregory, their little boy's first name. That's what it all said. But why?

95. "What the heck are you doing here?" I jerked around at the harsh, ugly sound of Steve's furious voice. I stared at him wordlessly as he strode over to the desk and snatched the incriminating policy

away from me, his eyes boring into mine like slits of steel. "I told Shirley to get it out of the file," he muttered, more to himself than to me. "I wanted to check something. But she shouldn't have left it —" His words filtered away as his rage turned from her, back to himself, and then to me again. "If you ever dare breathe a word of this to anyone, I'll —" His fists clenched and unclenched in a silent, futile threat.

96. The appalling words — common-law-wife — seemed to hang in the air between us like a black shadow. "You know I wouldn't," I whispered, finding my voice. "But why, Steve? I don't —"

97. "He was so anxious to protect them — against anything!" he grated. "He trusted *me*."

98. "Protect them against what, Steve?" I asked numbly.

99. He kept staring at me, as if he hated me. "Maybe if you understood —" he began. He ran his tongue across his lips and took a deep breath. Then the ghastly facts began erupting out of him in rough, choppy words. They'd both lived in a Texas city. Paul had been very unhappily married to a girl from a wealthy family — a girl who was an alcoholic and in and out of sanitariums.

Her father owned a huge electronics firm, where Paul worked as an engineer. After nine futile, unhappy years there were still no children, and Paul wanted out. But his father-in-law would not only not hear of a divorce, but he threatened to ruin Paul if he left his daughter or exposed her alcoholism.

100. Judy was a typist in the plant. They'd been thrown together and had fallen in love. When Judy got pregnant, they'd found the courage to cut all ties — family and friends — and even their identities and gamble together on a future without any security of any kind. For more than ten years they'd been safe. But Paul never stopped trying to safeguard the financial future of the girl he loved and their children.

101. "In case he died," Steve said. "Or was tracked down." He glared at me. "And now *you* know." He said it insultingly, and my eyes smarted with quick, furious tears.

102. "You must know I wouldn't tell anybody," I whispered.

103. The anger seemed to crumble right out of his face. "Okay, Laura," he said wearily, "I've got to believe you." He sighed heavily and added, "I'll be home around six."

104. I felt dismissed, and I drifted out, shocked and confused. I got to my car, sorry I'd found out. I didn't want to think about it, but I couldn't help myself. I couldn't get past the feeling of almost agonizing pity for Judy. How terrible it must be to have two children and no marriage, to live under such a secret cloud. But so many things were suddenly coming so clear. Now I understood their close-mouthed reserve with the rest of us, their careful, rigid economy, Judy's slavish devotion to Paul. No wonder she was so desperate to please him!

104 *thru* 113: *Element* VIII.

105. Her wistful words to Claire echoed back through my memory — "The only thing I really want is to keep Paul happy." She *had* to keep him happy, I thought with a fresh stab of compassion. She had no legal hold on him. She had nothing but his love, his *wanting* to be with her. I shivered at the thought of how hard it must be to have to keep a man feeling that way day after day, year after year.

106. It was ironic the way I ran into Paul — of all people — right then. I was stopped at the red light at Main Street when I saw him getting off the bus across the street. I sucked in my breath

and turned my head, praying he wouldn't see me. I couldn't face him — not right then. Out of the corner of my eye I watched for the light to change. I cringed as I saw him coming toward me, carrying a big bunch of daffodils. In the same second I got the light, I heard his voice calling out to me, and there wasn't a thing I could do. I had to look at him. I tried to get a smile on my face, and he climbed in. "I'm in luck," he said cheerfully. "It's a long six blocks."

107. I must have said something about his being early, because I remember his telling me he was taking advantage of a slack period at work to give Judy a hand with dismantling the kitchen for the big painting job tomorrow. I remember thinking I should tell him the job was done, then deciding it should be Judy's surprise. The only other thing I remember about those few minutes was his telling me about the daffodils, how there'd been a young boy selling them outside the office, and since yellow was Judy's favorite color, he'd had to get a bunch. I was so full of my guilty, secret knowledge about both of them that I couldn't even look him in the eye or trust my voice. I had to have

a chance to get used to it, I kept thinking, and then maybe I could be natural
with them again.

108. Judy had the door open and a bright,
welcoming smile on her face before I'd
pulled away. Through my rear-view
mirror I saw Paul running up the walk.
It struck me how different it was at our
house, with Steve usually late, usually
grumpy, with me dreading the inevitable scene over something one of the
kids had done or hadn't done or wanted
or some current difference of opinion
between us. There was always something. And the thought of Steve riding
on the bus with a big bunch of daffodils
in his hand was laughable — or it
would have been if it didn't suddenly
seem so sad.

109. Slowly I pulled into the driveway and
cut the motor, and then I just sat there,
letting my thoughts dart around in all
sorts of new directions. At least, I
thought, Judy *was* keeping him. And by
now Paul knew about the kitchen and
would be feeling very pleased. Now he
could play golf tomorrow, and Judy
would be happy about that.

110. "No woman should spoil a man like
that," Pat had said, and Claire and I
had agreed. But suddenly I was won-

dering if we were the ones who were
wrong. After all, it was Pat's husband
who was having an affair with another
woman. And we'd all secretly suspected
he wouldn't be coming home weekends
if it weren't for that marriage certificate.

111. Wasn't that what I'd meant when I'd
told Pat the wife always had the advantage? Wasn't it what Claire had meant
when she'd said, "After twelve years of
marriage men don't love their wives —
they're just stuck"? That was all Claire
had — a man who was stuck with her.
But he didn't approve of her, because
Claire believed in being what *she*
wanted to be, not what Gus wanted her
to be. Did Gus wish he weren't stuck
with her, I wondered. Then the devastating thought hit me. Did Steve wish
he weren't stuck with me? If he weren't,
would he *want* to stay with me?

112. The answer was painfully obvious, and
I got out of the car slowly, feeling sick
and scared. I walked into the house,
thinking about Steve and me and our
marriage in a way I'd never thought
about it before. I'd known Steve didn't
love me any more — certainly nothing
like the way he had when he'd asked
me to marry him. I'd thought it wasn't
possible — not after all the years and

struggling and children and daily problems. But it *was* possible. Judy had kept Paul's love because she had to. We hadn't had to. We had our legal marriage contracts to protect us. Our men were stuck, so we'd let down and stopped trying.

113. But suddenly more than anything in the world I wanted Steve to love me again — really love me the way he used to, enough to want to be with me whether he had to or not, not because he was stuck, but just because he wanted to. I thought about Judy again, and I knew what I'd have to do. I'd have to put my man first, ahead of everybody and everything, the way I used to when I was trying to get him to want me enough to propose. I'd have to be concerned with his happiness, not mine. I'd have to be the woman he wanted me to be and not the way I wanted to be. I'd have to be the way I was when we were going together — the way Judy was. And then, in the magical way of love, he'd want to share his happiness with me. Suddenly I saw how that worked, too.

114. I was still standing there in the middle of my living room, feeling excited and young and eager and wondering where

I could begin, when Terry burst in, looking furious. "You promised!" he shouted at me. "And now it's too late for Mr. Archer to get my name in!"

115. His camp application! I'd forgotten it again. I put my arm around him and hugged him tight. "You're going to have much more fun with us this summer, honey," I told him, suddenly knowing exactly where I was going to begin. "We're going to get a brand-new camper, Terry, and we're going to take a different trip every weekend. Daddy's going to show us how to cook over a campfire, and he's going to teach you how to cast in the brooks for trout, and how to paddle a canoe like the Indians did."

115 thru 117: Element IX.

116. He wrenched away from me, his eyes sullen. "But you said that wouldn't be any fun."

117. "I was wrong, honey," I whispered past the sudden lump in my throat. "So wrong about so many things." But I thanked God I still had time to start over. I had that precious marriage certificate that made Steve still feel stuck; I wasn't going to abuse it any longer.

118. It's almost fall now as I write this. It was a fabulous summer for all of us. It was often uncomfortable and inconvenient and never luxurious as we roughed

118: Preview para. (tell). 118 thru 123: Point 8 (Epilogue).

around the countryside, but I got what I wanted. Steve and I found each other again, and we found a richer, deeper love than we'd had in the beginning.

119. "I love you more now than I ever thought I could love anybody," Steve said last weekend while we sat in a rowboat on a little lake in Michigan, broiling under the sun after two silent hours of dangling our fishing poles without a single bite. And just when I was thinking that was about the most romantic thing a man could say to his wife of almost sixteen years, he chuckled and added smugly, "There's something about getting back to nature. You can't beat it."

119: *Preview* (*show*). 118 *thru* 120: *Element* X.

120. But I was thrilled all the same. Steve is happy now. He loves me, and I know now he's glad he's married to me. The kids are happier, too, because they now have a father their mother respects and appreciates and tries to please. We're enjoying being a real family now. But when they're grown and gone and Steve and I are alone again, we're still going to be in love, because I've learned now to keep it alive.

121. My only regret is that I haven't been able to help Pat and Claire — without telling Judy's secret, of course. I'd never do that. But I've tried to find another

121 *and* 122: *Point* 5.

way to make Pat see that what Wayne wants is to feel he is enough for his wife, that what he doesn't want is a wife who keeps making it so clear that any child is more important to her than he is.

122. And poor, frustrated Claire. She grabbed the chance to marry Gus, knowing he only wanted a substitute for the wife he'd lost. Then she resented that role and wanted a kind of love he no longer had to give. It was suddenly so easy now for me to see that if she'd been what he'd wanted and expected, the years could have turned his gratitude and contentment into a very real love just for her.

123. It all came down to the same thing again — putting your man's happiness ahead of your own. But Pat and Claire resent my new attitude toward marriage and my husband, and we don't see nearly as much of each other as we used to. I just hope my story will help other wives who have let love slip away from them because they refused to go more than halfway.

123: *Element VIII and Purpose (message for reader).*

— End —

CHAPTER XI

THE STORY BEHIND MY CHARACTER STORY

It was during a lecture on "INDIVIDUALITY" that I got the very first idea for this story. The speaker was talking about the uniqueness of every single human being and the reason for the individual's failure usually being the result of his measuring his worth against that of someone else. When he pointed out the fact that no matter how beautiful someone might be, there is always someone *more* beautiful — always someone stronger or richer or more talented or smarter to make that beautiful or strong or rich or smart one feel inferior after all — he convinced me that each one of us *is* a totally and forever unduplicated individual, each with his own rightful place and worth and potential success, not to be judged or evaluated by or compared with that of any other individual.

This Theme (ELEMENT VIII) intrigued me, because I personally was completely sold on it — and because so few people seemed to know it or live by it. And once I understood it, I couldn't help but see people all around me suffering from feelings of inferiority and failure because of this crippling, defeating tendency to judge their own assets and

137

accomplishments by those of others. Since it is such a common mistake, I knew it would make a great story with a lot of built-in reader-identification — and with a fresh and inspiring message.

Setting up the plot with two sisters, one the prettier, more talented, more popular, the other — my narrator, naturally, because *she* was the one with the wrong attitude (ELEMENT I) — the quiet, "inferior" one, an unhappy failure because she compared herself with her sister and, naturally (in line with my theme), she continually came out second best. I gave the girls names so I could feel I knew them better, calling the pretty one *Joyce,* deciding my narrator would be *Janet.* I wouldn't fall into the old cliche trap of having Joyce be the bad or the mean sister, and I could think of dozens of good, emotional, and significant incidents during their growing up years (ELEMENT II). I decided to sharpen Janet's long-range problem (*due to her flaw* — ELEMENT I) by having the girls' mother also be Joyce's type — self-confident, attractive, efficient, i.e., *successful!* And since the father in the story *naturally* adored and admired his wife, he would *naturally* approve of Joyce, the successful daughter who was following in her successful mother's footsteps. So now Janet was really up against a lot of stiff competition — *if* she was going to make the mistake most people make, allowing herself to be put down by others who didn't happen to understand or appreciate her unique assets.

I liked it. I loved my theme (ELEMENT VIII), and my flaw (ELEMENT I) was naturally the negative reverse. The motivation (ELEMENT II) for this flaw (ELEMENT I) would be easy. The problem (ELEMENT III) was a long-range one of inferiority, inadequacy, failure, unhappiness, which would logically progress into her fear of losing her man to the sister she feels inferior to, since the confession market likes man-woman stories. But I couldn't think of a climax (ELEMENT VII) that would give this story that "X" quality I felt it needed . . . Because, while the message in it seemed special to me, it came through too much like an illustrated article as it stood. It seemed too pedestrian, too lacking in the excitement of a good story. So I put what I did have into my IDEA file and proceeded along with other ideas, other stories.

It was in December, when I was shopping in the toy department for the children on my list, when I got that elusive, remaining piece for my plot.

In the crowded chaos of toys and kids and too many people, a small boy was nagging his mother for a Detective Kit he'd seen. I couldn't help overhearing a slightly older girl, obviously his sister, tell him, "Everybody has a different fingerprint. Did you know that, Jay? There are no two alike, ever."

"Tell Santa Claus," the distracted mother told him.

Outside, after I'd finished my shopping, I saw it had begun to snow. *And there are no two snowflakes alike either,* I thought, remembering the little boy who'd wanted the Detective Kit. And no two leaves or flowers alike, I remembered reading somewhere. And no two people!

That was when it clicked. It was when I remembered the half-finished plot. Now I had the missing piece — the climax (ELEMENT VII), that small incident (small in *this* story) that would logically show the narrator the philosophy I wanted to promulgate in this story.

I kept thinking about my new plot all the way home, and as soon as I got there, I jotted down the incident in the toy department, along with a few other notes to keep what I had fresh in my memory until I had a chance to get back to work in earnest . . . Notes like making my narrator a very sensitive, thoughtful girl so it would be logical for her to see this analogy.

I'm going to number these points now, so that, when I show you my plot, I will be able (by using the POINT NUMBER here) to show you how and where these noted ingredients were incorporated into my plot.

1. I'd have Janet married *so she could have a small child — to make this type of climax-incident logical and natural.*

2. I reminded myself that I'd have to show the reader (though Janet herself needn't understand it yet) that Janet was a successful person when she was herself — instead of a carbon copy of her sister. Otherwise my theme wouldn't be sufficiently proved! This meant that Janet would have to have had some successful years (of courtship and marriage) while she was separated from Joyce and, therefore, not forced into a position of doomed competition.

3. Then the trouble would start in again (*real* trouble as opposed to imagined, BUT only because of her flaw) when she's thrown back into Joyce's world.

4. This can be achieved by having her husband's job somewhere away from Janet's family — then a transfer, when *I'm* ready, can send them back again.

5. To make Joyce a real threat she'd have to be single; because after they've grown up and Janet's been married a few years, it's *illogical* for Joyce not to be married too. I could

let her be a widow, though — *hunting for a new husband!* (Not divorced, because then I'd have to give *her* a flaw and explain a lot of things that have nothing to do with *Janet's* story.) But I'd give her a child of her own. And this would not only come in handy (*two* small children) for my Detective Kit incident, but it would be a logical way to get Janet's husband involved with Joyce — because of the small, *fatherless* child (which I know now should be a *boy*), who, being Janet's husband's nephew, would provide a good excuse for his involvement.

As far as I could see then, without actually putting my pieces into the TEN ELEMENT pattern, my one remaining hole was the device part of the problem (ELEMENT III) — that incident that gives immediacy to the problem and forces the narrator to finally make a decision (ELEMENT IV) toward solving it.

I kept chewing at it, and I finally made my last note.

6. I will have Janet discover that Joyce and Chuck are actually having an affair. So she's forced to do something more conclusive than what she's done all her life: *suffer silently.*

It was a couple of days before I got back to it. But I had all the important pieces, and it was with a lot of enthusiasm that I put them all down into the ELEMENTS, which looked like this when I finished:

I. She thinks she's a failure, undesirable, because she can't keep up with her sister's successful performances.
II. Because her mother and sister were prettier, more popular, more self-confident than she, her father naturally approved of them and disapproved of Janet, so completely

different and lugging around a big inferiority complex that naturally makes her unattractive. After Joyce marries (*here comes Point One*), Janet gets a husband of her own and is thrilled when they have to move away, where (*now Point Two*), because she's free now of the constant unfavorable comparisons to Joyce, she lets herself BE herself and is, therefore, happy.

III.   However (*Point Four is taken care of here*), when her husband is transferred back, the old problem is not only upon her again, but it's aggravated by (*now Point Five*) Joyce's widowhood and fatherless son. (*Point Three here*) She stews along in her old, unattractive way (motivation for her husband's attraction to Joyce). DEVICE: She discovers (*Point Six coming now*) through an overheard conversation between the children that her husband is actively carrying on with Joyce.

IV.   To enlist her mother's help and then, with Joyce told to stay out of the way, she will try harder to be like Joyce, even though it means being unhappy and putting on an act. . . Because she believes this is the kind of girl her husband wants and needs.

V.   To keep her husband.

VI.   She never gets a chance to put her plan into action. So, while she takes care of both children, the stage is being set for the Detective Kit business — to pave the way for the climax. (This ELEMENT is unusually short in *this* story.)

VII.   This will be the scene between the two children discussing fingerprints, snowflakes, etc., with Janet overhearing them and joining in with her contribution of there being no two *people* alike, for that matter.

VIII.   And this is when she suddenly applies her own words

to her own situation and sees the theme: That no person can successfully emulate another, but can only be a poor carbon copy. . . Because each *is* unique and was created for his or her own individual place, ways, accomplishments, assets, etc., i.e., the message that should come through is: BE PROUD AND CONTENT TO BE YOURSELF!

IX. She offers him his freedom, since she is no longer going to try to be different from her real self and she believes he wants a woman like Joyce. Then she *acts* on the lesson she's just learned by refusing to do something he wants her to do, thus giving him up.

X. She gets him back, more solidly than ever now, because he does love and respect and admire her for what she really is — he just couldn't love or respect or admire a carbon copy *when he could have the real thing.*

❋   ❋   ❋

After a bit of trial and error, I decided to open my story with the introduction of the Detective Kit (though not the *use* of it yet), introducing all the characters and the situation and Janet's problem, *before* the Device (ELEMENT III), for two reasons. One, in *this* story there doesn't need to be any rush about the explanatory flashback (ELEMENT II) because the situation and the problem are so easy to make clear *without* all the detailed explanation — clear enough, that is, so that I can afford a leisurely opening; two, Janet's ghastly discovery (device) will carry more emotional impact if the reader has had a chance to get acquainted with these people and their relationships to each other and their situations *before* Janet shares the discovery with her. And a birthday party, with the Detective Kit one of the gifts, would be a good way to get the whole family together. So my opening is settled!

Because I am going to have a long, detailed ELEMENT II in this story, I am going to have to make a lavish use of PREVIEWS (as explained in Chapter VII on WRITING) to keep Janet's twenty-odd-year experiences from rambling interminably. And, as you read and study this story, I suggest that you keep in mind the fact that *this* story is strong on ELEMENT I (which *permeates* ELEMENT II, ELEMENT III, and ELEMENT VIII).

Chapter XII

"I COULDN'T DO THE THINGS MY MAN ASKED"

From: SECRETS (December 1969)

1. It was Kenny's seventh birthday that Wednesday night last August when my whole world fell apart. Kenny, my sister Joyce's little boy!

2. We were all over at Mom's — my husband Chuck and our little four-and-a-half-year-old Tammy, Mom and Dad, of course, and Joyce and her Kenny. Joyce's husband, big Ken, had been dead over a year — a year and four months, to be exact — and ever since last March, when Chuck and I had come back to San Francisco, Chuck had tried to be more than just an uncle to Kenny. "A boy needs a man to count on," he'd explained to me. And when I'd timidly mentioned Dad, he'd said, "A *young* man to *do* things with — until Joyce remarries, that is."

145

3. I'd had to go along with it. I hadn't   3: *Element* III.
liked it, but I'd tried to understand.
And, of course, Joyce would remarry. I
kept reminding myself I could count on
that. At twenty-six Joyce was as gorgeous
as ever, still a natural, delicate-looking
blonde, with a figure that made men
turn and stare. She was even more
clever and efficient and successful than
ever, if that was possible! And now that
she was over the grief period and actively looking around — well, of course,
she'd remarry. And I'd just have to wait
it out and pretend I didn't mind those
Saturday afternoons Chuck went over
to Joyce's on the pretext of being with
Kenny — to take him to the beach for
a swimming lesson or to a ball game or
for just plain man-to-man talks.

4. But my hurt and fear stayed sharp and
painful. Like that terrible Wednesday
night during Kenny's birthday dinner,
when Joyce had told us, "I'm letting
Kenny have the neighborhood gang in
Saturday afternoon for cake and ice
cream and games."

5. She shuddered daintily at the prospect,
and Chuck offered eagerly, "Maybe I
can come over and give you a hand."

6. Joyce accepted his offer just as eagerly,
and Mom and Dad innocently smiled

their approval. I hid my hurt because, as usual, nobody had said anything at all about Tammy and me coming, too.

7. Nobody noticed my silence, though, during the ice cream and birthday cake and the presents. There were lots of things besides the basketball set from Mom and Dad and the elaborate detective kit Chuck had picked out for Tammy to give her cousin — the two gifts that made such a hit with Kenny. Right away he'd turned to Dad with the plea, "Will you get it put up on our garage tonight, Grandpa?"

8. What had burned me was the quick, presumptuous way Joyce said, "Uncle Chuck will fix it for you Saturday, honey." And the enthusiastic way "Uncle" Chuck had agreed.

8 and 9: Element III.

9. It seemed like they were all against me, with Mom so complacently pleased with everything, with Dad beaming with relief and telling Chuck what a great guy he was. I blamed Joyce — I was sure she knew what she was doing to me! But I couldn't really blame Mom and Dad except for being so *blind* to what was happening.

10. When we finished, Kenny wanted to play with the detective kit, but Mom told him not to get into it tonight and

sent the two kids into the den — that had been turned into a playroom since Joyce had started working and leaving Kenny at Mom's during the day.

11. Dad took Chuck out to the garage to look over his new car, and the three of us, Joyce and Mom and me, got started with the cleaning-up process. I didn't even listen to their chatter, let alone contribute to it. I was too sunk in my own problem — how to keep my husband away from my sister! Or vice-versa!

12. When we finally finished, Mom asked Joyce to come upstairs to advise her about the length of her new dress. "Why don't you see what the children are up to, Janet?" Mom said to me. It was said with an unintentional, unconscious kind of contempt — the implication that my advice about *anything* was too worthless to bother with. I'd grown up with it, but it still stung. I smiled, though, not showing it, and drifted toward the den.

13. That was how it happened!   13: *Preview.*

14. For that first second I'd hesitated silently in the doorway, staring at them as they drew pictures on the big blackboard Dad had built for Kenny. He'd shot up so tall and straight. She looked

so tiny beside him, baby-rounded, with her blond curls.

15. Then Kenny glanced at the picture Tammy drew, and his disgusted voice spattered out. "No wonder your cat's no good. You're just a baby — you're not even five yet."

16. I thought it was cute the way Tammy thrust her chin up at him. "Well, I have a daddy, and you don't."

17. I gasped at the unexpected cruelty of her taunt. But before I could catch my breath to stop it, Kenny's retort was freezing me. "Your daddy and my mommy were wrestling on our couch last Friday night — and kissing, too, right at the same time." His voice had dropped to a confiding whisper, sounding only puzzled, not angry at all. "I didn't tell Mommy," he explained conspiratorially, " 'cause she gets mad when I get out of bed, and —"

18. "Show me how to make a pig," Tammy begged, bored with the subject and through with the heat of the argument.

19. I watched Kenny drawing and muttering instructions, while the meaning of his innocent words seared through me with a shocking horror. I stepped back, out of the doorway, hardly knowing I was doing it, the breath knocked out of

me. It was true! Joyce and Chuck "wrestling" on Joyce's couch, kissing — while little Kenny was supposed to be sound asleep.

20. I couldn't kid myself any longer. It was more than Chuck just being nice, more than the shadowy unreality of my insecure, frightened imagination. It *was* something real and bad. And the knowing now was like a match starting a brush fire in my memory. Last Friday night — that had been the night of the monthly executive meeting. It had been nearly two when Chuck had tiptoed in, reeking of liquor. That was what had wakened me. But he'd sounded so contrite when he'd explained the meeting had been extra long, then his immediate superior had taken a favored few of them to a bar to talk it over. I'd gone right back to sleep, reassured.

20 *and* 21:
Element III
(*device*).

21. But Chuck had lied to me! He'd been with Joyce! And they'd been making love — my pretty, talented, widowed sister and my husband, who wasn't satisfied with me any more.

22. I heard Dad and Chuck coming in the back door, and I managed to scuttle out of the way. I locked myself into the downstairs bathroom. I splashed cold water on my face and struggled to keep

breathing through the suffocating fear. All those Saturdays, all those evening office meetings, the "accidental" meetings at lunchtime, the looks and smiles and remarks right in front of me — Because they'd *liked* each other — I'd had to admit that much to myself. It *couldn't* be serious — I'd kidded myself about that. But now what? Now that I couldn't kid myself any longer —

23. I heard the heels clattering down the stairs — Mom's and Joyce's — and then all the voices mingling together in the living room, and I made a superhuman effort to pull myself together. I had to have a chance to think coolly and wisely before doing anything. And that meant I'd have to shut it out of my mind right now and keep it out until I did have that chance. I made myself take slow, deep breaths, then I put a smile on my face and walked out.

24. It was much, much later before I let myself think about it. It was after we'd gotten home and I'd tucked Tammy into bed. And after Chuck, not touching me at all except for the cool peck on the cheek, had rolled over and almost instantly begun the wheezy breathing that told me he was asleep. There was no sleep in me. There was just the fear

24: *Transition.* 24—*last two sentences*: *Flashback lead-in.*

and the rage and the jealousy — and the awful hopelessness. What *could* I do? What chance did I have? Joyce had always gotten everything she wanted. She had always *had* everything! Everything better than I.

25. In the very beginning, when I was very little, there'd been Joyce's two-year superiority. It was, "Ask your big sister." Or, "Take Janet along, Joyce." Or, "Joyce can do it; why can't you?" Or, "Joyce will show you how." Later on I saw that Joyce was prettier — showier. She had dimples, and she was a definite, bright, blue-eyed blonde. I was more vague — duller, ashy, gray-eyed. As we got into our teens, Joyce's figure filled out into exciting curves. I was just thin.

25 thru 33:
Element I.
25 thru 91:
Element II.

26. But it wasn't just the way we looked. It was *everything!* It was kind of like a vicious circle, with Mom being so pretty and smart and efficient and popular and sure of herself that naturally Dad thought she was perfect. And with Joyce being just like Mom, naturally they both approved of her. And with me being just the opposite — well, naturally they *didn't* approve of me.

27. So my life at home was a long series of failures and frustrations. Like Mom urging me to try out for the cheerleader

27: Preview

section — because Joyce had been a Pom-Pom girl when she was my age. When I tried to make her see that *I* wouldn't be any good at it, Daddy butted in and said, "Ask Joyce to give you some tips, honey."

28. There were so many times when one or the other of them would tell me to do it like Joyce did, to be like Joyce. The comparisons were endless, with me naturally always in the wrong. There was the humiliating time I overheard Mom asking Joyce to fix me up with a date for the Community Club Christmas party. Then, the next day, it was Joyce saying, "I'll get a guy for you, Janet, if you'll promise to talk — but about something besides some bird you rescued and nursed back to health."

28: *Preview*

29. There were so many times like that. There was one unforgettable Sunday morning when Joyce's gang met at our house so they could all take off together for their beach picnic. I could have killed Mom the way she hinted about me going along, until one girl finally did politely ask me. Naturally I refused, to the whole gang's obvious relief! But the minute they left, Daddy said disgustedly, "If you'd get your nose out of the books and *do* things with other kids,

like your sister, you'd be happier." I
wanted to tell him I'd be perfectly
happy if they'd all just leave me alone.
But I didn't. It was all I could do to
swallow down my tears.

30. None of them liked my friends — "no-
bodies," Mom called them. Joyce called
them oddballs. They were shy, non-
competitive bookworms like me, and
that's why I was comfortable with them.
But they were nice, and when I'd point
that out, Mom would say gently, "But
they're not popular, honey. They're not
the leaders." Like Joyce and her friends,
she meant. But neither was I!

31. I was sixteen when Joyce got married.   **31:** *Transition.*
It was the August after her graduation,
and everything about it was perfect.
The fellow, Ken Ferris, was handsome
and smart and a college graduate. He
had a good job with a big accounting
firm and a little legacy from his grand-
mother that made a nice down payment
on a darling split level house in Sausalito. So, as always, Joyce had it all —
the showers and the trousseau and the
big romantic church wedding with all
the trimmings, and the glamorous honeymoon in Acapulco.

32. I was happy for Joyce, and I'll admit I
hoped that now that she wasn't going

to be around all the time, my failures wouldn't be so noticeable to my parents. Not that either one had picked on me just to be mean or because they didn't love me. I knew that! It was just because I *wasn't* as pretty and successful and capable and everything else as Joyce, and I guess they figured their needling and criticizing would help me.

33. But nothing changed for me — not for those next two and a half years, that is. I kept on doing the best I could to make my parents proud of me, getting through school and graduating and getting a clerk-typist job with a plastics firm. That Christmas Joyce's little boy Kenny was going on a year-and-a-half, and big Ken worshiped her as much as ever. I didn't even have a boy friend!

33: Transition.

34. And then, a week later, I met Chuck Mitchell, and the big miracle happened — the miracle that was to change my life completely and make me truly, wholly happy for the first time in my life.

34: Preview.

35. It happened at one of those free-for-all, bring-your-own-bottle New Year's Eve parties a girl at the office asked me to at the apartment on Geary Street she shared with two other girls. "There'll be a bunch of guys from Berkeley," she

told me. "Don't you bring anything, though, Janet. There'll be plenty of booze. Just bring yourself."

36. I didn't want to go, without a date and knowing how lost I'd feel in a strange crowd. But I didn't have anything else to do, and Mom and Dad were going out, and — well, I just couldn't stand their pity at leaving me home alone on New Year's Eve. So I accepted.

36: *Element* I.

37. I was sorry the minute I walked into the smoky, noisy apartment, jammed full of beautiful, sexy girls and good-looking college fellows, all of them so uninhibited and so darn sure of themselves. They had a loud, hard rock record going full blast, and everybody seemed to be trying to talk over it. The bar was in the kitchen, and it was pure chaos. I kept slinking deeper into the corner, checking my watch. I'd leave, I kept telling myself, as soon as I could be sure Mom and Dad would be out. I'd just slip out and phone for a cab from the liquor store on the corner.

38. A miserable hour went by before I was able to get my coat out of the bedroom and escape into the hallway unnoticed. At least I thought no one had noticed me. But I'd no sooner punched the down button at the elevator than he

38 *thru* 44: *Element* I.

came after me — the tall, lanky boy, who stuck out his right hand and said, "I'm Chuck Mitchell."

39. I stared at him blankly, not offering my hand, not speaking. He had a drink in his left hand and a concerned frown on his face — and a half-shy, half-worried sound in his voice when he admitted, "I saw you sneak out." He smiled sheepishly, dropping his hand. "You can't do that."

40. "Why can't I?" I demanded. "I hate crowds," I added, punching the elevator button again.

41. "What you need is a drink," he said lamely. "Nobody should be alone on New Year's Eve."

42. His pity was unbearable — and so were the tears that blurred my eyes. "How can it possibly concern you?" I cried, turning toward the stairway and blindly hurrying down the two flights. While I stumbled along, clutching onto the bannister, I heard the rattle of the ancient elevator. But it didn't matter any more, and I didn't think about it.

43. I got to the lobby just as the elevator stopped — and Chuck Mitchell stepped out, without the drink and with an embarrassed flush on his face! "I hate crowds, too," he said pleadingly.

44. I looked at him, and I giggled unexpectedly. He grinned his relief and took my arm. "I've got a car across the street," he said. And I smiled up at him, suddenly terribly glad he'd followed me.

45. It was a crazy and wonderful and ridiculous evening. We drove around awhile, just talking, getting acquainted. Chuck had more to tell. He was twenty-three, originally from Seattle. His mother had died the fall of his senior year, and when his father remarried the following spring, he enlisted right after graduation. When he got out of the Army, he started in at Berkeley on a G.I. loan. He'd pushed it, working, studying, taking summer courses.

45: Preview.

46. Now he was getting his degree in engineering in three-and-a-half years, graduating next month. "And just last week," he told me, "I signed up with Terrascience, for five years in the field."

47. I heard the enthusiasm in his voice, and I knew Terrascience was a big, important geoscience company, with field crews stationed all over the Southwest. I didn't understand then, though, exactly what it meant. But when he said, "So I'll be leaving for the Panhandle around the first of March," I did understand that, and I felt a prick of regret.

48. Everything about that night was different from any other date I'd ever had. It was all so unplanned, and both of us were so comfortable with each other and having such a ball eating hamburgers and fries at an ordinary drive-in on New Year's Eve! The most unusual part of it all was the way *I* talked to *him,* not just about the facts about myself and my family, but the honest things — like my real reason for being at the party tonight and my real reason for leaving it. "I just don't project," I confessed while we drove aimlessly through Marin County. "That's what my sister tells me."

49. "You sure project with me, honey," he said, tightening his arm around me.

50. It was past two when Chuck dropped me off at home. All those hours, with nothing happening at all, I marveled. Or had everything happened? He touched my lips with his in a sweet, soft kiss, and he said matter-of-factly, "Can you be ready by one tomorrow, Janet?"

51. "Easily," I said breathlessly.

52. "I'm glad we began this new year together," he said huskily. "Because now I know it's going to be a great one for both of us."

53. "So do I," I whispered.

54. It was like magic, the unbelievable way   54: *Preview.*
his prophecy came true. It was a quick,
wild, whirlwind romance, with the two
of us only really aware of each other,
even when we were with others or my
parents or Joyce and Ken. They all liked
Chuck — how could anybody help it?
— but Mom and Dad didn't want us to
rush into anything. "Wait," they said,
"and be sure."

55. But Chuck had to go way down to   55: *Transition.*
Texas, and he wanted me to go with
him. And, oh, how I wanted to! So we
didn't even argue with them. We quietly, secretly got our license and tests
and were married in City Hall. Mom
was disgusted, telling me what a fool
I'd been to sacrifice all the fun — the
parties and the wedding and the gifts.
Like Joyce had had! And what a mistake I was making now to waste the
five best years of my life in a trailer
camp in a Texas dust bowl! Neither
Mom nor Joyce could understand why
I wouldn't try to talk Chuck out of it.

56. The truth was I was glad to escape all   56: *Element I.*
the fuss. All I cared about was being
Chuck's wife. So for once nothing they
said put the tiniest dent in my happiness. I was secretly glad we were going
to bury ourselves in a small, faraway

place where I wouldn't have to try to live up to all the things I wasn't. I loved Chuck so much, and I wanted him all to myself.

57. I had five glorious years of pure happiness and overflowing love. I loved our trailer, one of two hundred. I loved the company "town" that was really just an enormous trailer park, with its huge community building in the center to serve all of us. I loved the other young families and the whole roughing, crude, pioneer kind of life we all led in the dusty, hot, freezing, windy oil country. I loved living in jeans and shirts and boots. I reveled in the isolation of our own settlement that kept us all so close, like a big family, but without the kind of female competition I'd grown up in. I loved the closeness with Chuck and our long evenings alone together, talking about his work.

57: Preview. Also, Point 2 in previous chapter.

58. Like the other engineers, Chuck started out as a junior field engineer, which was really an assistant to the boss of that particular crew. The whole idea was to locate oil deposits in new areas, with most of the gamble of wildcatting removed, and the more I listened and learned about it, the more the fellows' excitement rubbed off on me. They

worked from off-road vans, which were full of fascinating geological and electronic equipment, and lots of times they were way off in areas as far away as New Mexico for days at a time. But I was never lonesome. I had all my wonderful new friends, and after the baby came, I had her to take care of and to love and play with.

59. Even though the housework was at a minimum, there was always plenty to do, because there was always so much going on, with our various committees constantly organizing pot-luck dinners and bingo games and square dances and talent shows. I blended contentedly into the background of it all, happy to work behind the scenes, and nobody expected me to do or be anything I couldn't do or be. I guess it was because nobody tried to impress anybody else.

60. There was one bad time for me that second Christmas when we went home with Tammy. I was scared and miserable every second we were there, with Joyce and Mom and their probing questions and their terrible sureness about everything. In all the secure happiness I'd forgotten how it used to be — how it was again, with me feeling unattractive, unsure, a failure. I was glad we

60: *Preview.*

weren't there long enough for Chuck to notice, and I was thrilled to get back home to our trailer. After that I found all kinds of excuses to keep from going back for other visits.

61. After three years Chuck got his promotion to full-fledged field engineer, in charge of his own outfit, and as Tammy grew, so did my joy. One of my favorite jobs in the trailer park was taking charge of the preschool children. I loved reading to them and stretching their wonderful little imaginations — with finding pictures in the cloud formations or acting out nursery rhymes or tending our flower garden and watching things grow.

61: Character Plant to motivate Element VIII.

62. Once Chuck said, "With you and Tammy I've got the whole world. What did I ever do to get so lucky?"

63. But I was the one who'd gotten so lucky!

64. The shocking news of Ken's death in April, eleven months before we were due for a transfer, was the one big, tragic blot on the beautiful years. It was so sudden and unexpected we could hardly believe that big, husky Ken's heart had given out under the anesthetic while he was being operated on for kidney stones. Ken was only twenty-eight. Little Kenny wasn't six yet.

64: Plant.

65. It was so sad, and I felt so sorry for Joyce I'd have done anything I could to help. But what could I do? Chuck and his crew were on a five-day field trip in New Mexico, and Tammy — three then — was down with the chicken pox that had spread through our trailer park like a brush fire. So I couldn't even go to the funeral.

66. But as the weeks rolled by and summer came Mom wrote that Joyce was snapping out of her grief quicker than she'd hoped and was taking hold of her life again. Luckily Ken's affairs had been in good shape, and a mortgage insurance policy had cleared the house for Joyce and Kenny.

67. That fall Mom's letters were full of Joyce's exciting new job as receptionist for a big, travel agency. It was Kenny's first year of school, and Joyce had registered him in our old grade school, a block from Mom's, so he could go right to Mom's after school was out and Joyce could pick him up on her way home from work. "It's all working out so nicely," Mom wrote. "Now, if you and Chuck would get transferred back, everything would be wonderful." I didn't say so, but I prayed we wouldn't.

68. So my heart sank that next March when   68: *Element* I.

Chuck's orders came — because it was back to San Francisco. "As a junior executive," he exulted, so obviously thrilled I couldn't let him know how it scared me. "I'll be a liaison man," he explained excitedly, "between headquarters and the field crews. I'll learn to schedule their operations and handle logistics and see that supplies and spare parts are in the right place at the right time." He ran out of breath and picked me up and swung me. "And even more money, Janet," he gloated. "Aren't you glad?"

69. "Of course," I said. And I had to pretend to mean it.

70. Mom and Dad insisted we stay with them while we went house-hunting. Chuck had made very good money during the five years we'd been gone, and we'd spent very little of it. So the down payment wasn't any problem. But everything else was!

70—last two sentences: Preview.

71. Everything! Just being around Joyce and Mom again, seeing them in action, always looking so marvelous, managing everything with such smooth, poised efficiency, made me shrivel inside of myself. And there was the way Mom and Dad kept advising Chuck about living up to the job he had now if he

wanted to go to the top. It meant establishing himself in the right background and doing a lot of entertaining, they warned us both. It meant putting up a good front all the way around. "A man's family and home life are as important in business these days," Dad told Chuck, "as his job performance."

72. There was the night at dinner when Joyce said critically, right in front of everybody, "You're going to have to get a whole new wardrobe, Janet, now that you're back in the city."

72 thru 76: Element III sharpens.

73. Mom's eyes raked over me as she agreed. "You look dowdy, Janet."

74. What really hurt, though, was Chuck telling me later that night, when we were alone, that he wanted me to get a lot of new things. "Good things, honey," he said. "You know, real stylish."

75. I smiled past the hurt that lumped up in my throat. Was he ashamed of me now? And then he made it so much, much worse. "Why don't you get Joyce to go along with you, Janet?"

75 and 76: Element I.

76. I remembered our first date when I'd told him how inferior my sister had always made me feel, and I wondered how he could have forgotten. I thought of reminding him. But I was suddenly afraid to point out my shortcomings, so I tried not to let him guess how I felt.

77. Chuck was busy breaking into his new job, but we kept spending our evenings and weekends looking for our house, finally whittling it down to two choices. One Joyce had found for us in her area, in Sausalito. It was built into a hillside, with no yard at all for Tammy, jammed in with other expensive houses. It was modern and pretentious, with its sunken living room and built-in bar and glamour bathrooms. I hated it! But Joyce and Mom had convinced Chuck it was ideal for business parties, and Chuck was suddenly all for business — and suddenly all for Mom's and Joyce's opinions!

78. "It looks like a place for an affair," I complained to Chuck, "not a family."

79. "We're in the city now," he reminded me unnecessarily.

80. I loved the other one — the older, frame, two-story house way out in San Rafael. It was like a country town, slow-paced, woodsy and rustic, with the houses on big lots. The house we could have had had a gorgeous ancient redwood in the middle of its big fenced yard and a huge, old-fashioned birdhouse that fascinated Tammy. There were fruit trees and a sturdy elm for a swing. The friendly, older couple next door were working in their vegetable garden the two evenings we drove out

80: *Character Plant to motivate Element* VIII.

to look at it, and I knew they'd be wonderful neighbors.

81. But Chuck wasn't drawn to it the way
I was. "It's too far," he complained.

82. "It's only twenty miles farther," I said,
"less than a half hour's driving time. It
just seems farther," I added wistfully,
"because it's such a change."

83. In the end we moved temporarily into
a very modern, very fashionable, very
jazzy, very expensive furnished apartment on Nob Hill. It was supposed to
be temporary, but we stayed on and on,
through the spring, into the summer —
while I tried with all my heart and soul
and might to be the kind of wife Chuck
needed now. The kind who could be a
good hostess and a popular guest.

84. I tried! But I could write a book about   84: *Preview.*
my failures. Like the time I spilled a
drink on one of the bigwigs because my
fingers were icy cold and shaking from
nervousness. And the time I drank one
too many and laughed too shrilly at
something nobody else laughed at.
There was the time it was our turn, in
our apartment, and I burned the can-
apes Mom had brought over with careful instructions to heat them under the
broiler for one minute. But Tammy had
called me, and I'd forgotten. They'd

caught on fire, and the smoke and smell filled the living room. And there were all the times I talked too much or was too silent.

85. Everybody was always politely kind. But I couldn't get close to them. They were too polished for me, too competitive, the women too sleek, the men too aggressive. I couldn't play their game, and I was afraid of them.

86. There were so many occasions. There were the office get-togethers. And the sophisticated partying crowd in the building. And Joyce's gang! I even took bridge lessons, but I always managed to commit several unforgivable goofs. Chuck tried to be patient with me at first. And then he began not even trying. He'd tighten up on the way home and snarl, "Couldn't you have pretended to get the joke?" Or, "Did you have to sulk in the corner all evening?"

87. I don't know exactly when he began comparing me with Joyce all the time — or exactly when I knew they were really attracted to each other and I was so scared because they were together so much of the time. I kept trying to reassure myself. It was because of Kenny, I told myself, and because Joyce liked men — and now she didn't have one of

87: *Element* I *and Element* III.

her own. And because I was such a flop!
So I tried harder to be what Chuck
wanted me to be, and I tried not to
worry about Joyce.

88. But I kept on worrying about everything. I brooded about our sex life — or
rather, the increasing lack of it. In
Texas our physical love had been so
heavenly, so fulfilling. But that was because our love had been so untarnished.
We'd approved of each other then; we'd
been happy. And making beautiful love
had been as natural and perfect and
automatic as breathing. Now without it,
I felt more and more stifled, nervous,
scared. It was no wonder Chuck rarely
reached for me any more — no wonder
those infrequent times he did left us
both exhausted and unsatisfied.

89. Sometimes when I was alone, I'd catch
myself thinking about the house in San
Rafael, imagining how it would have
been if we'd bought it and were living
there now. Maybe Chuck would have
been more contented, less involved
with this fast-paced, social life that
seemed so phony and meaningless to me
and that I couldn't seem to fit into. But
we hadn't bought it, and I always had
to come back to the frightening question — where were we going from here?

90. The only times I was happy that summer were the healing times I was with Tammy — and sometimes Kenny, too, when Mom had other plans — and was too busy and involved with them to think about myself. Worried and unhappy and helpless-feeling as I was that summer, though, it never occurred to me that Chuck could actually be making love to Joyce.

90—last sentence: Flashback lead-out.

91. But I was sure of it that Wednesday night of little Kenny's seventh birthday, when I'd overheard him telling Tammy that he'd seen her daddy and his mommy wrestling and kissing on the couch last Friday night. Kenny had been puzzled, because he was too young to understand. Tammy was too young to care.

92. But blind and stupid as I was, I'd known then. And I'd stood there in the doorway, paralyzed with shock, unnoticed by the chattering children. Somehow I'd gotten through the rest of the evening without anyone noticing there was something terribly wrong with me — wrong, like a suddenly broken heart!

93. But later, as I lay wakeful and tense beside my sleeping husband, feeling like a prize fool for not realizing long ago what was going on, the old self-dis-

93: Back to opening.

gust scalded over me, hotter than ever. Why *would* they notice how crushed I was when they were used to my failures?

94. I brooded about it all that next day, Thursday, still not knowing what to do. I had to face it now for what it was — an affair. And I had to do something. I was afraid to tell Chuck I knew, though. What if he told me he was glad I knew — because he wanted to be free of me and just hadn't known how to tell me? I thought of going to Joyce and humbling myself and frankly begging her not to take him away from me. I would have — if I hadn't been so afraid she'd ask me, in her kind-sounding, superior voice, how I could want to hang onto a man who no longer loved me.

94: Element III (device).

95. I was glad Chuck brought home some papers to work on, and after I tucked Tammy away and cleaned the kitchen, I went to bed, still not knowing what to do.

96. But when Mom called early Friday afternoon to tell me she had to have her hair done at four for the Chaneys' dinner party and could she drop Kenny off at my apartment after school for an hour I said, "Of course." And I suddenly knew then what I was going to do.

96: Element IV.

I was going to tell Mom about it, and I was going to ask her to help me! And I knew she would. Maybe Mom didn't think I was as pretty or as smart or as clever as Joyce, but she loved me just as much. And she was always trying to help me, wasn't she? She wouldn't let Joyce take Chuck away from me. I didn't know *how* she'd manage it, but I knew she would.

97. I felt as if an unbearable weight had slipped off my shoulders all the while I was getting Tammy up from her nap and dressed and waiting for Mom. I'd have another chance now. And somehow this time I would make good. Somehow I would be the kind of wife Chuck needed, and I would make him happy.

97: *Element V.*

98. Mom was in too much of a rush to get to the beauty shop when she dropped Kenny off to give me the chance to talk then, though. But I didn't worry about it. Maybe I'd have the chance when she picked him up later. If not, I'd go over there tomorrow. I was so relieved at having made a decision I didn't scold Kenny for bringing his detective kit with all the messy ink pads. I just spread an old blanket over the pale carpeting where the two kids had settled down and let them go to it.

98—*last two sentences: Plant.*

99. Even now it still seems strange to me the way it took such a little thing to suddenly change the whole course of my life after twenty-four years of going along in the same blind, defeated, frustrating direction.

99: *Preview* (*tell*).

100. The "little thing" that got it started was hearing Tammy's piping baby lisp telling Kenny, "But mine is different." As I moved closer with a tray of cookies and milk for them, I saw the paper they were staring at, with the smudged fingerprints on it.

100: (*show*)

101. "'Course they're different." The male superiority in Kenny's voice amused me. "Everybody has different fingerprints from everybody else." He looked up and saw me. "Don't they, Aunt Janet?"

101 *thru* 104: *Element* VII.

102. "That's true," I told Tammy, setting the tray down. "And it's true with leaves and snowflakes and flowers," I rambled on, warming to my subject. "And ears, too." I'd heard that somewhere. "Everybody's ear is different from everybody else's."

103. Even Kenny was impressed now, I noticed. "But there's so many people," Tammy objected, fingering her little ears and staring at Kenny's, then at mine.

104. I laughed at her tiny concept of "so many people." "And they're all different, too," I said.

105. That was what was so funny — the way
I sat there on the floor with them, thinking about my own words. "And they're
all different," I'd said—all the people,
in all space, in all time.

105: *Element*
VIII

106. That meant me, I thought wonderingly.
And Joyce! And Mom! That meant we
were all different from each other. We
were supposed to be different! Because
that was the way God had planned His
universe, with infinite variety, with no
duplications. Everybody knew that.
Even I had known it. I'd just never put
it together right.

107. But now that I was finally putting it together, I was suddenly seeing the absolute futility of my trying to be like
somebody else — like Joyce, for instance, the way I had all my life. No
wonder I'd kept stumbling and failing
and sinking deeper into the depression
of inferiority. And no wonder I'd been
so happy those five heavenly years in
Texas — because for that too-brief time
I hadn't had to try to live up to a better
person than I was, because the very sim-
plicity of the life itself had let me be
myself, without criticisms or comparisons.

108. But those years were gone, I reminded
myself, and I was back in the city,
where Chuck's ambitions and my sis-

ter's attractions were showing me up for what I was. And no matter how I tried and pretended and imitated, I was still *me* — not the kind of woman Chuck wanted now! And no matter how I tried, I was never going to be able to make myself into somebody else.

109. I got up off the floor, so filled with grief and heartache I was hardly aware of the children. I knew I was going to have to let Chuck go! As I moved heavily into the kitchen, I began discovering something else — that stirring through the misery there was a kind of peace in the failure. I guess it was the peace that comes from facing facts, from getting off a merry-go-round that can only spin in a get-nowhere circle. I knew at last that never, ever again, not for any reason or any person, no matter how I loved him, was I going to struggle against my own nature.

109: *Element* IX.

110. There was a painful lump of sorrow deep inside me when Chuck got home for dinner, but on the outside I was controlled and determined. Mom had come and gone with Kenny, and I'd managed to keep her from suspecting I'd just come to the dead end of my marriage. While I fixed dinner, I thought about **Tammy**. Naturally it was going to make

a difference to her, not having a father an everyday part of her life. But it couldn't be helped! I'd do everything I could to keep her from being cheated. I'd let Chuck visit her and have her with him as often as he wanted to. I'd never criticize him or Joyce in front of her. No matter how it hurt or what it cost, I'd do everything I could to make it up to her for being *me*.

111. Chuck didn't see anything different about me, either. Not that he looked! He strode in, perspiring, dropping the coat he'd been carrying and brushing past me in his hurry to get a cold beer.

112. I watched him sickly, loving him so much and knowing how much I was going to miss him, but knowing, too, how much happier he was going to be with Joyce.

113. He took a deep gulp, and then he gave Tammy a big bear hug. Then he turned to me. "The Brodies are having two tables of contract bridge at their place tonight," he told me, sounding pleased about it. "I told Allan we'd be there around eight, so you'd better get on the phone for a baby-sitter."

114. "No," I heard myself saying. "I'm not going, so — " I saw the startled, open-mouthed way he was looking at me,

114: *Element* IX.

suddenly seeing me, and, oddly, it gave me the extra spurt of strength I needed. "I hate bridge," I said quietly. "And I don't really like the Brodies or their friends." I bit my lip to keep from telling him I knew about Joyce now and I was going to give him his freedom. I didn't want to get into it till we'd had dinner and I'd gotten Tammy to bed.

115. I turned back to the stove, but he grabbed my shoulders, whirling me around. "What are you talking about?" he demanded, his voice rough, his eyes accusing. "*You* don't like *them*?"

116. I shrugged out of his grasp. "We'll discuss it after dinner," I said coolly.

117. He turned and clumped into the living room. A second later I heard him dialing, then his muffled voice. I held my breath, straining to hear. I couldn't make out the words, but I knew he was telling the Brodies we weren't coming, and I wondered dully what excuse he was giving. I heard him hang up, and then I heard the television blare into life.

118. I stalled as long as I could with my chores and rehearsed my speech over and over, but by eight there was nothing left to do except go into the living room and puncture Chuck's grim, wait-

ing silence with the words that were
going to break my heart.

119. He looked up sullenly when I walked
in and sat down on the sofa across from
him. "I know about you and Joyce," I
said flatly in a thin voice. I had to look
away from the shocked, guilty flush that
spread over his face, and then, before
he could ask how I knew, I pushed out
the rest of it. "And it's all right. I'm
willing to give you a divorce." I waited,
my throat aching with unshed tears, my
mind clutching at the things I was going to say next if he tried to deny it or
if he got defiant and defensive, telling
me how *I'd* failed *him*. I was ready for
anything — I thought.

119: *Element*
IX.

120. But Chuck didn't say those things. He
cleared his throat and swallowed a few
times. And then he said in a scratchy
voice, "I can understand why you'd be
— mad." He shook his head as if he
could shake the confusion out of it. "I
don't blame you," he grunted. "But how
can you — stop loving me? So quickly,
I mean," he finished in a hoarse whisper.

121. "I haven't stopped," I said. "It's just that
I don't blame *you*, only myself. But I
can't compete or pretend any more! I've
got to be *me*."

121: *Element*
VIII.

122. He looked so blank I knew I was going

to have to explain how it all happened. So I took a deep breath and plunged in. I told it in a fast, choppy rush — how I'd overheard the kids last Wednesday night, how it had all added up. I reminded him of our first date when I'd told him what a failure I'd always been, growing up in the shadow of my prettier, smarter sister, constantly trying to keep up, constantly failing.

123. I stopped, but he kept waiting. So I started in again. I told him why I'd loved the years in Texas. I told him how miserable and frightened I'd been in the five months we'd been back in San Francisco. I'd only kept trying and bumbling along because I loved him so much. "But after what happened this afternoon," I wobbled along, "I found out I *can't* be somebody else. All I can be is *me!*"

124. His eyes kept boring into mine. He didn't move a muscle. He didn't even have any expression at all while I told him how the discussion about the fingerprints had made me see it all so clearly.

125. He didn't say a single word till I'd said it all. Then he groaned, "I'm sorry, Janet. I didn't understand. I forgot — " His voice cracked. "I'm just so sorry!"

126. It was over! He knew I knew, and he was sorry. And now we both knew why our marriage had failed and why there was no hope for it. I stood up, feeling too drained to discuss the details. Tomorrow was Saturday. We'd have the whole day to work things out — and get him packed and out. "I'm going to bed," I said woodenly.

127. He nodded, letting me go, sitting as still as if he'd been carved out of stone. I felt like a lump of stone myself as I walked into the bedroom.

128. I hurried out of my clothes and into bed. I felt as weak and lifeless as a rag doll. Even if I hadn't known Chuck wouldn't come near me tonight or any other night, I wouldn't have worried. I was too exhausted. All I wanted was the oblivion of sleep for a little while.

129. But sleep wouldn't come. My mind wouldn't stay still long enough. Would Chuck phone Joyce tonight to tell her it was all clear for them now? Or would he go to her? But there weren't any sounds in the living room. Was he worrying about Tammy? Or crippling alimony? I'd have to go into that with him tomorrow, I reminded myself. I'd have to tell him I *wanted* to share Tammy — for her sake! And I would want to go

129: *Element* IX.

back to work, so I wouldn't want any more money from him than I'd have to have for Tammy.

130. Was he thinking right now of the awkwardness of swapping wives right in the same family? My harried thoughts spun around distractedly. What would Mom and Dad think? I couldn't even guess. I'd move — to one of the older, inexpensive apartments on Russian Hill, near Mom's. I was going to need her now, too, for a little while, with Tammy still so young.

131. The clock kept ticking, louder and louder, and the silence in the living room stretched ominously. And I stayed as wide awake as ever. He'd probably fallen asleep on the sofa, I thought.

132. Hours went by while I turned and twisted and kept trying to blank out my mind. I finally gave up and lay limp and spent, waiting for dawn.

133. And then I heard the muffled sounds from the living room, the heavy, padded footsteps coming closer, and I sucked in my breath. I couldn't cope with any more tonight. But he came on into the bedroom, and then his shadowy bulk was standing over me.

133 thru 147:
Element X.

134. "Are you awake, Janet?" he whispered softly.

135. "Please," I cried. "Please — I can't talk any more tonight."

136. "I've got to tell you now, honey," he begged raggedly. "I've been such a fool — such a blind, stupid, selfish, rotten jerk!" His voice fogged up, and I wondered achingly if he was crying. Then he sank down on the edge of the bed, his hand coming out to find mine.

137. "I love you, Janet. I never stopped loving that real you, honey. I just — forgot —" His words choked off again, and he grabbed me, burying his face in my shoulder, his hands trembling against my back. "I don't know why we all thought you should be more like Joyce. I don't know why I went along with that in the first place."

138. My own arms came around his neck with a volition all their own, and we lay there, close, our hearts racing together. I didn't understand what was happening. I just knew my love was close to me again after such a long, frightening, lonely time, and right then that was all that mattered.

139. "But I can see now," he went on, "why I thought Joyce —" He broke off, but I knew what he meant — why he thought Joyce was superior. "But that was only because the real item is always

better than the counterfeit." He laughed shakily. "That real you is the one I want, Janet. Will you be that girl again, and will you give me another chance to prove my love, darling?"

140. I tightened my arms and raised my lips for his. It was all the answer he needed. And after that, for those next glory-filled minutes, neither of us even thought. We only felt the rush of our love sweeping us together into a wild, dizzying crescendo of passion that rocketed us together up to our old private heaven.

141. "Let's have a picnic tomorrow up in Marin County," Chuck said to me later in a low, sleepy voice.

142. "But Kenny's party," I remembered suddenly. "You promised Joyce — "

143. "She'll manage," he cut in. Then eagerly, "And we can see if that house in San Rafael is still for sale."

144. I guess it was my need for more reassurance, or maybe it was just the perversity of being a woman that made me whisper, "But it's so far from the company."

145. "Look," he said gruffly, "I'll do a good job for them, but my private life is my own." He hugged me, without passion now, but with so much love. "And if

they don't like it, then I guess I can always get another good job, huh, Janet?"

146. "You can do anything, darling," I said fervently.

147. We stayed close all night, Chuck's arm across my shoulder, my body nestled into the curve of his, and I knew the exact moment he fell asleep. It was another few minutes before I drifted off — just those few minutes it took me to feel the wonder and joy of being *me!* Me, unlike anybody else, not superior to anyone but not inferior, either. Just myself, unique! Me, the girl Chuck had fallen in love with — the girl he still loved, I thought exultantly. I was so thankful I was *me!*   THE END

147: *Element* VIII.